This Book Belongs To

_____

AWESOME!

AWESOME!

EXPLORING THE NATURE
AND NAMES OF JESUS

DICK EASTMAN

Chosen

a division of Baker Publishing Group
Minneapolis, Minnesota

© 2021 by Dick Eastman

Published by Chosen Books
11400 Hampshire Avenue South
Bloomington, Minnesota 55438
www.chosenbooks.com

Chosen Books is a division of
Baker Publishing Group, Grand Rapids, Michigan

Printed in China

Library of Congress Control Number: 2021930312

ISBN 978-0-8007-6195-0 (cloth)
ISBN 978-1-4934-3130-4 (ebook)

Cover design by Studio Gearbox

21 22 23 24 25 26 27   7 6 5 4 3 2 1

FOREWORD

HAVE ONLY A FEW HEROES. Dick Eastman is one of them. The first time we met, the humility and authority with which he prayed floored me. I mean that literally. I ended up on my knees in prayer!

There is an authenticity to Dick Eastman's life and leadership that is too rare these days. When I think of Dick, I am reminded of Acts 4:13: "They took note that these men had been with Jesus" (NIV). If there is a secret to Dick Eastman's intimacy with God and impact on the world, I think that's it. He spends a lot of time with Jesus! And when you do that, you become a lot like Him.

The book you are about to read, *Awesome!*, is going to stretch your faith. It is not just well written, it is well lived. There are insights into who Jesus is that can be learned only by long obedience in the same direction. I love books that share the "latest and greatest" research on a subject matter. Can I tell you what I love even more? Hard-earned truth from someone who has "been there and done that."

I love spending time with people who know God better than I do. Why? Because it fuels my hunger for God and stretches my faith. That is this book. It will help you follow Jesus a little better, a little closer.

The apostle Paul said, "Follow me as I follow Christ." The same could be said of Dick Eastman, of this book. In the pages that follow, may you rediscover who Jesus is all over again! At the end of the day, it's all from Him and it's all for Him. He is the all in all. When you get to the final page, I trust that your life will be more than ever submitted to His Lordship.

Mark Batterson, *New York Times* bestselling author,
The Circle Maker; lead pastor, National Community
Church, Washington, D.C.

ACKNOWLEDGMENTS

AM DEEPLY INDEBTED to those who helped make possible the thoughts shared in the pages of this book. I particularly thank Steven Kipp, Jordan Middlebrook and Dena Jefferson for their editorial assistance as well as their many hours researching the insights of historic Christ followers and church leaders who passionately sought to know and serve Christ with total abandonment. To Tanner Peake and Tim Middlebrook, Every Home for Christ's executive director and senior vice president respectively, I am especially grateful for their anointed leadership as my wife, Dee, and I look back at more than 32 years of leading this global ministry. God has graciously sent men like these to help lead the Every Home ministry into a glorious future to reach every home on earth with the timeless message of this book, that Jesus Christ is not only awesome, but the only way to eternal salvation. To David Bryant I offer special thanks for being such an encourager to me personally to pursue an intimacy of knowing Christ in a depth I never could have imagined when I first came to know Jesus nearly six decades ago. Finally, to the more than 8,000 global staff of Every Home for Christ in 189 worldwide offices, and the more than 100,000 monthly volunteers in the field, I joyfully honor and thank you for taking the message of Christ's love to some 350,000 homes daily. This labor of love has always been and will always be *all about Jesus!*

Dick Eastman

A CALL
to the HEIGHTS

So, my dear Christian friends, companions in following this call to the heights, take a good hard look at Jesus. He's the centerpiece of everything we believe.

HEBREWS 3:1 MSG

SOMEONE HAS SAID, "If you want to get in good with God, brag on His Son!" Here goes!

It all began with a question from a friend—this personal quest to explore the wonders of the nature and names of Christ.

David Bryant, author of the classic volume *Christ Is Now*, all 608 pages exalting the Person of Jesus Christ, was speaking to the staff of Every Home for Christ, the ministry I lead. I had invited David to our ministry headquarters, The Jericho Center in Colorado Springs, Colorado, to spend a day in prayer with me. Because our staff begins each day with a time of corporate prayer and worship, I asked David if he would share something from his heart that morning concerning his life's calling. Then, as a staff, we would gather around him to pray for God's blessing on his calling. Of course, I was certain everything we would hear in those moments from David would be about Jesus!

Our Core Identity

David did not disappoint. He began by quoting Swiss professor Karl Barth, one of the most influential theologians of the last century. Barth would often challenge his students: "Show me your Christology and I'll tell you who you are!"[1] Christology, of course, is the study of the life of Christ, or the theology of the Person of Jesus Christ. Bryant paraphrased Barth's words suggesting, "What you think about God's Son is the single most important thing anyone can know about you." Bryant further explained, "In a profound sense, the core identity of any Christian must never be separated from his or her vision of Jesus Christ. That's because Christ is the core identity of Christianity itself!"

Bryant then asked our staff: "What do *you* think about God's Son?" I could almost hear the corporate minds of our staff, the majority of whom are under the age of 35, silently responding: "He's really cool," or even, "He's awesome!" Everyone in the room, of course, knew that Jesus was the reason for our ministry's existence. For one thing, it's in the very name of the ministry—Every Home for Christ. We often say our name is our mission. Everything we do is about Jesus. Our goal is to take the good news of Christ's love to every home on earth.

But what David proposed next in his brief message that morning brought pause to most if not all in the room. It was a challenge for each to engage in an imaginary exercise. It was meant to help everyone stop and think about how well we actually knew who Jesus is—right now. That simple exercise profoundly affected me. For days afterward it was on my mind almost constantly. I had been in the crosshairs of David's challenge. In fact, it has led to the writing of this book. Here's how it unfolded. . . .

Captivated by a Challenge

Bryant shared:

> Imagine you have just been invited by the most popular radio talk show, a worldwide talk show, to answer a single question. Your response would go global. Billions will hear. You will have three minutes to speak to the entire world about Jesus. The talk show host then gives you the question and hands you the microphone. The question: "Who is Jesus Christ right now?" Your head spins for a moment. You do recall how Jesus asked a similar question of His disciples centuries ago. It's recorded in Matthew 16:13: "Who do men say that I, the Son of Man, am?" (NKJV). Now it's your turn to tell the whole world.

David amplified the question by suggesting the radio talk show host asks you: "How would you describe God's Son in terms of all that He is at this present moment?" He then adds a bit of clarification to the experiment:

> Keep in mind, your goal is not to tell the listeners about who Jesus was in the past during His earthly ministry; nor is it to tell about who He will be someday when He returns in His glory, but who He is right now. Further, you're not being asked to explain what Jesus has done for you personally, as wonderful as that has been.

David further explains: "You see, this isn't about you. Whether you or I exist is irrelevant. You're to describe simply who Christ is as the

Person of God's only Son, exalted at this very instant as Sovereign Lord over heaven and earth!" I knew our staff had been captivated by the challenge, as was I.

Later, after spending a better part of the day with David praying in one of the numerous prayer grottos at our ministry headquarters, The Jericho Center, I mentally went through that simple exercise. Here I was, leading a ministry sharing the Good News of Jesus with as many as 350,000 families every day, at their doorsteps, in 150 nations, and I saw myself stammering and stuttering at an imaginary microphone trying to describe who Jesus is to me, right now, for just three coherent minutes on a worldwide radio broadcast. What followed over many months was a desire to get to know the Jesus who changed my life six decades ago in a much fuller and richer way—now!

Becoming a Christ Explorer

David Bryant's challenge soon led me into a yearlong pursuit of exploring the wonders of the nature of Christ. With scraps of folded paper in my pocket at all times throughout each day, whenever I thought of a new descriptive adjective picturing the nature or character of Christ, out came those scraps. Soon I was adding passages of Scripture that highlighted these qualities to my growing list. The scraps grew and multiplied! Jesus was taking center stage in my life. Or was it that I was moving step by step toward joining Him at center stage of His life? I am sure it is the latter.

I realized I couldn't put everything I scribbled down to later expand and compile into a practical devotional book unless it approached the size of Tolstoy's *War and Peace* (all 1,225 pages). So what follows is a bit of a primer. A definition of *primer* reads, "A textbook giving the first principles of any subject" (*Webster's New World College Dictionary*).

This book is barely a beginning—which brings to mind the apostle John's concluding words to his gospel: "And there are also many other things that Jesus did, which if they were written one by one, I suppose that even the world itself could not contain the books that would be written. Amen" (John 21:25 NKJV). That is not hyperbole. One might ask, What "other things" was John talking about? How about the stars, for example? Yes, Jesus created them. There is Scripture to prove it. And He gave them all names. I'll speak about that in a later chapter, even describing how many millions of libraries it would take just to contain a listing of all those stars, and their names, that exist in known space. And who knows what might exist beyond known space? (Of course, I think we both know who knows!)

Enough said! Or should I say *not enough said*? Would you join me daily in exploring the wonders of the nature and names of Jesus? Let's begin by spending a "Month in the Son" together. Just one month to begin with. Perhaps after that, this could become a monthly habit. If you need to stretch it out longer than a month at the start, that's fine. *Bask in the Son as long as you like*. If you discover something new about Jesus not on my lists (whether it concerns Christ's nature or His names in Scripture that I might have missed), email me your discovery at Jesus@everyhome.org.

But critical to our journey—before we get started I need to explain to you our two main objectives for the journey: first, to "*magnify* Christ's nature," and second, to "*glorify* Christ's names."

Dick Eastman,
Colorado Springs, Colorado

A MONTH in the SON

Magnify His Nature!

> The Son is the dazzling radiance of God's splendor, the exact expression of God's true nature—his mirror image! He holds the universe together and expands it by the mighty power of his spoken word.
>
> HEBREWS 1:3 TPT

To sum up the Son is not an easy thing to do! But I feel compelled to try! After Mary, the mother of Jesus, received the promise of the coming Messiah from the angel Gabriel (Luke 1:28–49), she sang: "My soul magnifies the Lord, and my spirit has rejoiced in God my Savior. . . . For He who is mighty has done great things for me, and holy *is* His name" (verses 46–47, 49 NKJV). To *magnify* is "to make greater in size, status or degree." Our English word *magnify* comes from the Latin *magnificare*: "to make much of" or "to esteem highly."[1] A. W. Tozer said, "You can't make God big but you can see God big!"[2] As together we spend a Month in the Son, our goal is to see God big through the prism of His Son.

In the pages that follow, we will explore the wonders of the nature and names of Jesus. Each day we spend during our Month in the Son, a chapter will help us explore the wonders of a foundational aspect of Christ's nature and character. Each chapter will then be followed by a list of names and phrases of the Lord from Scripture (for meditation, praise and prayer) that describe the wonders of all Christ is to His followers. (More about these lists of names, and how to apply them in daily prayer, will be shared in a moment.)

The primary goal in the pages ahead is both to explore and to experience the awesome wonder of Jesus Christ in new ways. *Wonder* by definition is "a person, thing, or event that causes astonishment and admiration." Jesus is the Person who causes astonishment and admiration. Wonder is likewise "the feeling of surprise and awe aroused by something unexpected or incredible." Jesus is full of awe-inspiring surprises and incredible blessings for His followers. He is the essence of astonishment and admiration. Quite simply, Jesus is *awesome*!

As you turn the pages that follow, may I suggest that you are not reading a book as much as embarking on a journey? I will be making that journey with you. And when we get to the end, we will discover it is just the beginning. *But first, some very important words about exploring the wonders of Christ's names.*

Glorify His Name!

> "The syllables of your name murmur like a meadow brook. No wonder everyone loves to say your name!"
>
> Song of Songs 1:3 MSG

Why do the Scriptures share so many different names or descriptive phrases of the Lord? Luis de Leon, Augustinian friar and theologian (1527–1591), offers a most interesting observation. Of course, living in sixteenth-century Spain, Leon lacked the many Bible translations and other resources we have today. Yet, from his knowledge of Scripture, he wrote: "Christ is given so many names because of his limitless greatness and the treasury of his very rich perfections and with them the host of functions and other benefits which are born in him and spread over us. Just as they cannot be embraced by the soul's vision, so much less can a single word name them."[3]

As you seek to glorify the names of Christ daily, keep in mind that a simple dictionary definition of *name* reads: "a word or words by which an entity is designated and distinguished from others." The many expressions describing Christ in the chapters that follow clearly distinguish our Lord from all others. Andrew Murray, in his classic work, *With Christ in the School of Prayer*, wrote:

> What is a person's name? It is a word or expression in which a person is represented to us. When I mention or hear a name, it brings to mind the whole man, what I know of him, and also the impression he has made on me. . . . His name is the symbol of his power. And so each name of God embodies and represents some part of the glory of the Unseen One. The name of Christ is the expression of everything He has done and everything He is and lives to do as our Mediator.[4]

My Anchor in Jesus

A delight of my daily prayer times over the years is to have discovered the significance of bringing these names of the Lord into my devotional times from day to day. This began four decades ago, when I initiated a habit of keeping a daily journal. That habit continues to this day, almost fifteen thousand entries later (in multiple three-ring binders).

Several months into developing this journaling habit, I began noticing in my daily Bible readings numerous descriptive phrases describing our Lord—the promised Messiah. I began compiling a list of these names and phrases that I would refer to often in my daily times of prayer. Soon thereafter, another habit emerged—that of writing into my journal one of those names or phrases daily, claiming that specific expression (and what it conveyed) as my anchor in Jesus for that day. Over ensuing years, and using a typical "through-the-Bible annual reading guide," I have read and prayed through various translations of Scripture, which significantly expanded my list. I would frequently notice the nuanced ways various translators would describe the wonders of our Lord's names. Before long, I organized the list alphabetically and ultimately compiled it in a 31-day format. Also of note, although numerous expressions on the daily lists in this book come from the Old Testament, keep in mind that God was "in Christ" (2 Corinthians 5:19) and that any reference to "the Lord" in the Old Testament also refers to Christ. Paul made it clear that all the "fullness" of the Godhead dwells bodily in Christ (Colossians 2:9).

The day-by-day listing that follows, consisting of 868 names or expressions describing our Lord, is the result. Because they are presented in a 31-day format (with a daily list following each chapter in this book and its specific theme), you can select some or all of that day's list as fuel for prayer, praise and meditation. To merely read through an entire list prayerfully for a particular day, pausing to highlight one or two names you specifically claim as significant for that day's challenges, is easily done in five minutes or less. If you see a specific name that has special meaning for you that day, you might circle it and write the date beside it. And if you do this monthly, you won't come back to that day's list for another 31 days. By then it will be like starting afresh if you decide to make this a continuing habit.

I suggest doing this in your daily quiet times of prayer for at least several months just to see how such a habit might impact your prayer life. To me, this is worth sacrificing some of your usual television watching, social networking or other Twitter-consuming moments that too often occupy significant portions of our days. Wise is the statement I heard recently: "Facebook proves that Christians in America have plenty of time to spend in prayer." And as you meditate on the nature of Christ and the wonders of His names, consider adding your own characteristics, thoughts or qualities about Jesus to your personal list as they come to mind. Ask yourself the question, "Who is Jesus to me this very day?" Let me know what you discover afresh by emailing me at Jesus@ everyhome.org.

Going Deeper

At the conclusion of each of the 31 main chapter themes on the nature of Christ that follow, I suggest four practical steps to go deeper in your pursuit of these qualities, including ways to apply the names of Jesus listed for each day:

1. **Explore:** To *explore* means "to look into closely; examine or search carefully; investigate." In your daily quiet times, meditate on that specific day's primary theme describing Jesus. Specifically, meditate on one or more of the passages of Scripture in that chapter.

2. **Experience:** To *experience* involves any "activity that includes training and knowledge, skill, or practice resulting from such activity." Pray specifically for a personal revelation of how each day's quality of Christ relates to your life, family or others in your sphere of influence. Take this theme into your day. You may wish to write down one of the Scriptures in this lesson to memorize throughout the day.

3. **Express**: To *express* is "to put into words; to picture; to give expression to one's feelings or imagination." During your daily quiet times, consider investing five to ten minutes to journal your thoughts as they relate to that day's theme. This will provide you a source to return to daily to record your impressions as you spend your Month in the Son. This could well begin a habit that lasts a lifetime. And think about this—it's all about Jesus!

4. **Exalt:** To *exalt* means "to praise; glorify; extol—to raise on high; elevate, lift up." Devote a portion of your daily prayer encounter to verbally glorify the Lord. You can pray, praise, meditate or even sing through each day's list rather easily, and even in just a few minutes of time. And as suggested earlier, keep a pen nearby and circle any specific name you wish to claim that day, even noting the date by that name. Remember, Jesus told His disciples to "ask anything in my name" and He would respond (John 14:13-14).

THE
SUPREME
JESUS

Exploring the Wonders of Christ's Supremacy

Christ is to the souls of men what the sun is to the world. He is
the center and source of all spiritual light, warmth, life, health,
growth, beauty, and fertility. . . . Like the sun, He is free to all. All
may look at Him, and drink health out of His light.

J. C. RYLE

SO THIS IS JESUS!
We begin at the conclusion. And the conclusion is really just
the beginning. As we begin our journey in exploring the wonders of the nature and names of Jesus, there is nothing more central
to our quest than recognizing and pursuing the supremacy of Jesus
Christ. He is first and foremost the *Supreme Jesus*. I suggest the beginning is the conclusion because, in the end, one can say nothing more
than that Christ is fully, categorically and emphatically *supreme*. He is
supreme from the outset, He will be supreme through every aspect of
our journey, and He will be supreme in the end. And of course, there
really is no end! Eternity is forever, and Christ is eternally supreme!

In our quest to know Christ more intimately, as together we spend
a Month in the Son, we will quickly realize there is no theme we might

address concerning Christ's nature, character or essence that is not cause for adding the qualifier *supreme*.

Further, to amplify these qualities, we will explore, pray and praise our way through the many names and phrases that describe our Lord in Scripture—all 868 that I have catalogued over the years from multiple Bible translations during my prayer times. And the summary of it all is the unimaginable, incredible, indescribable, incomprehensible supremacy of Christ. As John R. W. Stott wisely wrote: "The riches of Christ are unsearchable. . . . Like the earth, they are too vast to explore, like the sea, too deep to fathom. They are untraceable, inexhaustible, illimitable, inscrutable and incalculable. What is certain about the wealth Christ has and gives is that we shall never come to an end of it."[1] But that won't stop us from pursuing Him! Oh, dear friend, there is so much more!

The Centerpiece of Everything

What exactly do we mean by "supreme"? *Supreme* simply means "most excellent; highest in rank, power and authority; utmost; ultimate; superior." Synonyms for *supreme* abound, and each aptly applies to the *Supreme Jesus*. Some include paramount, matchless, unrivaled, unparalleled, unsurpassed, unequaled, unexcelled, dominant, indomitable, omnipresent, preeminent, unsurpassable, flawless, incomparable, exceptional, invaluable, and magnanimous.

The writer to the Hebrew believers uniquely highlighted Christ's supremacy in declaring:

> So, my dear Christian friends . . . take a good hard look at Jesus. He's the centerpiece of everything we believe, faithful in everything God gave him to do. Moses was also faithful, but Jesus gets far

> more honor. . . . Moses did a good job in God's house, but it was all servant work, getting things ready for what was to come. Christ as [God's] Son is in charge of the house.

HEBREWS 3:1–6 MSG

To refer to Christ as the "centerpiece of everything" is to speak of His supremacy. In writing to the Ephesian believers, Paul admonishes: "So now you Gentiles are no longer strangers and foreigners. . . . You are members of God's family. Together, we are his house, built on the foundation of apostles and the prophets. And the cornerstone is Christ Jesus himself" (Ephesians 2:19–20 NLT).

Here Paul clearly states that the *cornerstone* is Christ Himself. A key definition of *cornerstone* reads: "The basic, essential, or most important part; the foundation." A cornerstone for a new building typically represents a stone that forms part of the corner of a building, especially a foundation stone, usually inscribed with the date and other details of the placing of the stone. Most often a cornerstone is placed in a building during a ceremony that marks the building's beginning. This adds to our definition of the supremacy of Christ. He is not only the beginning of the building; He is the building itself.

Supreme over All!

The supremacy of Christ cannot be overstated. It is, as I have suggested, the beginning and the conclusion, and everything in between. It is the reality of all realities! Dietrich Bonhoeffer, most remembered for his definitive book *The Cost of Discipleship*, wrote: "In Jesus Christ the reality of God entered into the reality of this world. . . . Henceforth one can speak neither of God nor of the world without speaking of Jesus Christ."[2]

Perhaps Scripture's most significant insights on the supremacy of Christ are found in this passage from the apostle Paul's letter to the Colossian believers:

> Christ is the visible image of the invisible God. He existed before anything was created and is *supreme over all creation*, for through him God created everything in the heavenly realms and on earth. He made the things we can see and the things we can't see—such as thrones, kingdoms, rulers, and authorities in the unseen world. . . . He is the beginning, supreme over all who rise from the dead. So he is first in everything.
>
> Colossians 1:15–18 NLT, *emphasis added*

Especially make note of Paul's use of the word *everything. Everything* means just that—*every thing! Everything* is defined as being "all that exists; all that relates to the subject; and all that is important." As someone wisely said, "All means all and that's all 'all' means!"

Charles Spurgeon was arguably one of the greatest pulpit orators of all time. He was known for saying he would take any text from the Bible and proceed immediately to the cross. Highlighting his convictions on the supremacy of Christ, Spurgeon once told his congregation, "I sometimes wonder that you do not get tired of my preaching, because I do nothing but hammer away on this one nail. With me it is, year after year, 'None but Jesus!'"[3]

And that will basically be the theme of our journey together as we enjoy our Month in the Son! Jesus is everything! He is supreme! He is extraordinary. He is incomparable! When our journey is completed, may our heads spin in wonder, reverence and delight as one word comes to mind: *Awesome!*

A PRAYER FOR TODAY

Jesus, my supreme Lord and God, I humbly bow before You today. I recognize Your ultimate supremacy over all things in heaven and all things on earth. God, I know that in Your fullness You chose to live as Christ. Through Him, You reconciled everything to Yourself—including me! Your Son, indeed, is the centerpiece of everything: everything we believe, everything we long for, everything we live for. Search my heart today, oh Lord. I want You to reign supreme in my life just as You reign over all creation. May every part of my life be wholly submitted to Your supremacy. In Your supreme name I pray, Amen.

Encountering the *Supreme* Jesus:
A PRACTICAL APPLICATION

Remember—these four steps, as explained more fully on pages 23–24 in the introduction, are suggested to help you apply this quality of Christ to your own life.

1. **EXPLORE:** Take time to meditate on this quality of Christ. Use Scriptures in this chapter to get started.

2. **EXPERIENCE:** Turn your meditation into prayer that this quality might impact your life today. Pray the above prayer to begin.

3. **EXPRESS:** During your quiet time, take a moment to journal your thoughts, even if briefly.

4. **EXALT:** Pray, praise or even spontaneously sing your way through today's list of the names of Jesus. It only requires a few minutes.

GLORIFY HIS NAME

Those who know your *name* trust in you, for you,
LORD, have never forsaken those who seek you.

PSALM 9:10 NIV, *emphasis added*

A to Z Revelation 1:8 MSG

Adonai-Jehovah (Sovereign Lord)
Genesis 15:2, 8 NLT

Advocate, An 1 John 2:1 NKJV

Alive Forevermore Revelation 1:18 NKJV

All and in All Colossians 3:11 NKJV

All I Want in Heaven Psalm 73:25 MSG

All I Want on Earth Psalm 73:25 MSG

All That Matters Colossians 3:11 NLT

Almighty One, The Revelation 1:8 NLT

Alpha and Omega Revelation 1:8 NIV

Altogether Lovely
Song of Solomon 5:16 NKJV

Always and Ever Sovereign
Psalm 102:12 MSG

Amazing Counselor Isaiah 9:6 MSG

Ancient of Days, The Daniel 7:13 NKJV

Angel of His Presence, The
Isaiah 63:9 NKJV

Anointed Leader, The Daniel 9:25 MSG

Anointed One 1 Timothy 2:5 TPT

Apostle and High Priest of Our
Confession, The Hebrews 3:1 NKJV

Arm of the Lord Isaiah 51:9 NKJV

Armed and Battle-Ready
Psalm 24:8 MSG

As Rivers of Water in a Dry Place
Isaiah 32:2 NKJV

Assurance of Glory Colossians 1:27 NLT

Astonishing Gift 2 Corinthians 9:15 TPT

Atoning Sacrifice for our Sins
1 John 2:2 NIV

Attorney Job 16:19 MSG

Author and Finisher of Our Faith,
The Hebrews 12:2 NKJV

Author of Eternal Salvation, The
Hebrews 5:9 NKJV

Author of Life, The Acts 3:15 NLT

THE
AWESOME
JESUS

Exploring the Wonders
of Christ's Awesomeness

Be sure . . . that your faculty of wonder is used in holy things; let your astonishment bless God.

CHARLES SPURGEON

SOME QUALITIES OF CHRIST'S NATURE and character, His very essence, we can only observe. Other qualities we can emulate. For example, we can desire to be more compassionate, humble, prayerful or selfless. These are but a few of the qualities of Christ we will look at in the pages that follow. However, some aspects of Christ's essence we might describe as "wonder qualities." For example, we cannot emulate (i.e., strive to imitate) His supremacy. We cannot seek to be more *supreme* as we might seek to be more *compassionate*. We can only observe and encounter Christ's supremacy. The same can be said about His awesomeness. We cannot be more *awesome*. He alone is awesome and supreme in these and every other quality we might examine of His essence. But we can live out the implications of these unique qualities of our Lord, day by day. Today we focus on the *"Awesome Jesus"*!

Awesome beyond Words

Awesome by definition means: "Awe-inspiring; exalted, wonderful, re-markable, extraordinary; magnificent." This describes a person or experience that is stirring or deeply moving. *Awe* is defined as "a feeling of fearful or profound respect or wonder inspired by the superiority or grandeur of a person."

How awesome is Jesus in your life right now? Do you see Him as awe-inspiring, wonderful, extraordinary and magnificent? The psalmist gave us this challenge: "Be in awe before his majesty. Be in awe before such power and might! Come worship wonderful Yahweh, arrayed in all his splendor, bowing in worship as he appears in the beauty of holiness" (Psalm 29:2 TPT). Elsewhere the psalmist declared: "The Lord God Most High is astonishing, awesome beyond words!" (Psalm 47:2 TPT).

The purpose of the pages that follow is to help you see Jesus in all His awesome wonder. *Wonder* by definition, as briefly mentioned in my introduction, is "a person, thing, or event that causes astonishment and admiration." How awesome is Jesus in your life? Do you long to have a life-altering encounter with the awesomeness of Christ? Puritan revivalist Jonathan Edwards describes just such an experience:

> In 1737 I had a view, that for me was extraordinary, of the glory of the Son of God as Mediator between God and man and His wonderful, great, full, pure and sweet grace and love, and meek and gentle condescension. This grace appeared ineffably excellent with an excellency great enough to swallow up all thought and conception. . . . I felt an ardency of soul to be, what I know not otherwise how to express, emptied and annihilated; to lie in the dust and to be full of Christ alone.[1]

Sheer Wonder

Reflect with me a moment on the ancient biblical account of Samson. Most remember Samson for his dying moments when, having been blinded by his enemies after he lost his powers due to disobedience, God restored his strength, and he tore down the temple of Dagon. More of the enemy died in that instance than had died by Samson's hand the rest of his entire life.

But go back with me prior to Samson's birth when a heavenly messenger described as "the Angel of God" delivered a promise to the household of Manoah, Samson's future father. Manoah's wife had been childless—apparently for years. The Angel of God appeared first to Manoah's wife. "I know that you are barren and childless," this divine being declared, "but you're going to become pregnant and bear a son" (Judges 13:3 MSG). This visitor suddenly disappeared as Manoah's wife rushed to Manoah to tell him of the promise.

"A man of God came to me," she exclaimed, adding, "He looked like the angel of God—terror laced with glory!" (verse 6 MSG). She then recounted how this divine being had given her a promise just before he disappeared: "You're pregnant. You're going to give birth to a son. . . . The boy will be God's Nazirite from the moment of birth to the day of his death" (verse 7 MSG).

Manoah prays that this supernatural visitor might return to teach him and his wife how to raise this promised Nazirite child. His prayer was answered, and the Lord does return, appearing once again first to Manoah's wife. Again his wife leaps to her feet and rushes to Manoah, declaring, "He's back! The man who came to me that day!" Manoah quickly returns with his wife and asks this supernatural being for further help in raising the promised child. Before the Angel of God departs a second time, Manoah has a final question: "What's your name? When your words come true, we'd like to honor you." The Angel of God's response is terse but telling: "What's this? You ask for my name? You wouldn't understand—it's sheer wonder" (Judges 13:17–18 MSG).

Delightfully Mysterious

Manoah and his wife lacked the Scriptures as we have them today—God's holy Word, the Bible. What an anointed resource to help us explore and experience the awesome wonders of our Lord! May we respond daily to the psalmist's challenge: "Now, with breathtaking wonder, let everyone worship Yahweh, this awe-inspiring Creator" (Psalm 33:8 TPT). To this, we heed the additional invitation: "Drink deeply of the pleasures of this God. Experience for yourself the joyous mercies he gives to all who turn to hide themselves in him. Worship in awe and wonder" (Psalm 34:8–9 TPT).

Are you ready to be astonished? Before we continue our journey, the psalmist adds this additional observation: "For God's mighty miracles astound me! His wonders are so delightfully mysterious that they leave all who seek them astonished" (Psalm 111:2 TPT).

I know we are but scratching the surface in trying to explore the awesomeness of Jesus. And the surface is myriad wonders deep! But together, let's go deeper!

A PRAYER FOR TODAY

Awaken me, Lord Jesus, to Your goodness inhabiting all things. Awaken me to Your presence in my life and those whom I may encounter today. Awaken me to Your awesome creation. Awaken me to Your awesome wonder that I might bring You greater glory. Awaken me to Your grace in every moment of my day. Capture my attention, Jesus, so that I may spend all my days in astonished awe of You. Amen!

Encountering the *Awesome* Jesus:
A PRACTICAL APPLICATION

Remember—these four steps, as explained more fully on pages 23–24 in the introduction, are suggested to help you apply this quality of Christ to your own life.

1. **EXPLORE:** Take time to meditate on this quality of Christ. Use Scriptures in this chapter to get started.

2. **EXPERIENCE:** Turn your meditation into prayer that this quality might impact your life today. Pray the above prayer to begin.

3. **EXPRESS:** During your quiet time, take a moment to journal your thoughts, even if briefly.

4. **EXALT:** Pray, praise or even spontaneously sing your way through today's list of the names of Jesus. It only requires a few minutes.

GLORIFY HIS NAME

I will be glad and rejoice in you; I will sing
praise to your *name*, O Most High.

PSALM 9:2 NIV1984, *emphasis added*

Avenger Jeremiah 51:36 MSG

Avenging God Psalm 94:1 MSG

Awe-Inspiring God Psalm 76:7 TPT

Awesome in Your Sanctuary
Psalm 68:35 NIV

Balm in Gilead Jeremiah 8:22 NKJV

Banner for the Nations, A
Isaiah 11:12 NKJV

Beautiful Crown, The Isaiah 28:5 MSG

Bedrock on which I Stand, The
Psalm 144:1 MSG

Bedrock under my Feet Psalm 18:1 MSG

Beginning, The Colossians 1:18 NLT

Beginning and the End
Revelation 1:8 NKJV

Beginning of the Creation of God,
The Revelation 3:14 NKJV

Best, The Psalm 95:3 MSG

Best Picture of God
2 Corinthians 4:4 MSG

Bishop of Your Souls 1 Peter 2:25 KJV

Blessed and Only Almighty God,
The 1 Timothy 6:15 NLT

Blessed and Only Potentate, The
1 Timothy 6:15 NKJV

Blessed and Undisputed Ruler
1 Timothy 6:15 MSG

Bouquet of Wildflowers
Song of Solomon 1:14 MSG

Branch of Righteousness, A
Jeremiah 23:5 NKJV

Branch of the Lord, The Isaiah 4:2 NLT

Bread from Heaven, The John 6:51 MSG

Bread of God, The John 6:33 MSG

Bread of Life, The John 6:35 NLT, MSG

Breathing Room for My Soul
Psalm 62:6 MSG

Bright Morning Star, The
Revelation 22:16 MSG

Brighter Than the Brilliance of a
Sunrise Psalm 84:11 TPT

Brightness after Rain 2 Samuel 23:4 NIV

THE
BEAUTIFUL
JESUS

Exploring the Wonders of Christ's Beauty

When you hear the voice of Jesus saying, "Come to me," pray that God would give you eyes to see Jesus as irresistibly true and beautiful.

JOHN PIPER

O VER THE YEARS, my life has been profoundly impacted by mighty giants of the faith whose lives have challenged me to pursue God in greater dimensions. One of those is Robert Murray McCheyne, a Scottish preacher in the mid-nineteenth century who was passionately consumed with the beauty and wonder of Christ. Referencing Song of Solomon 5:16, McCheyne introduces us to the *Beautiful Jesus*:

> You will never find Jesus so precious, as when the world is one vast howling wilderness. Then He is like a rose blooming in the midst of the desolation, or a rock rising above the storm! Do not set your hearts on any of the flowers of this world. They shall all fade and die. Prize the Rose of Sharon and the Lily of the Valley. Jesus never changes. . . . Yes, He is altogether lovely. This is my Beloved, and this is my Friend![1]

Dazzling Radiance

Today we turn our attention to the wonders of Christ's beauty. How beautifully do you see Jesus right now? The apostle Paul wrote to Corinthian believers: "Remember, our Message is not about ourselves; we're proclaiming Jesus Christ, the Master. All we are is messengers, errand runners from Jesus for you. It started when God said, 'Light up the darkness!' and our lives filled up with light as we saw and understood God in the face of Christ, all bright and beautiful" (2 Corinthians 4:5–6 MSG). The author of Hebrews adds: "The Son is the dazzling radiance of God's splendor" (Hebrews 1:3 TPT). This is beauty to the extreme!

The psalmist likewise spoke about the beauty of the Lord. He wrote: "For God is sheer beauty, all-generous in love, loyal always and ever" (Psalm 100:5 MSG). Elsewhere he declared: "For GOD is great, and worth a thousand Hallelujahs. His terrible beauty makes the gods look cheap. . . . Royal splendor radiates from him, a powerful beauty sets him apart" (Psalm 96:4, 6 MSG). King David, in one of his most memorable psalms, wrote: "I'm asking GOD for one thing, only one thing: to live with him in his house my whole life long. I'll contemplate his beauty; I'll study at his feet" (Psalm 27:4 MSG).

Meditate for a moment on this expanded definition of *beautiful*: "the quality attributed to what pleases or satisfies the senses; having or possessing beauty; qualities that are especially attractive." Synonyms include "loveliness; elegance; magnificence; excellence, attraction, fascination; majesty; value; merit; worth and allurement."[2] Indeed, there is no single word or phrase in any definition of *beautiful* that cannot be applied to our Lord.

Occupied with Jesus!

Few historic church leaders have fascinated me as much in their radical devotion to Christ as has Francis of Assisi. Born the son of a wealthy Italian merchant in the late twelfth century, and living only 44 years, Francis forsook all of his inheritance at the age of 27 and founded what would become the Franciscan Order. This humble Italian friar left such a legacy that generations would know him simply by the city of his birth, as Francis of Assisi.

What most marked Assisi's life was his pure passion for Jesus! He was consumed with the beauty of Christ. Such was evident when he wrote to his fellow Franciscans about his beautiful Savior:

> We should wish for nothing else and have no other desire, we should find no pleasure or delight in anything except in our Creator, Redeemer, and Savior; He alone is true God, perfect, good, all good, every good, and the true and supreme good . . . loving and gentle, kind and understanding.

In this same discourse, Francis elaborated:

> Nothing, then, must keep us back, nothing separate us from him, nothing come between us and him. At all times and seasons, in every country and place, every day and all day, we must keep him in our hearts, where we must love, honor, adore, serve, praise and bless, glorify and acclaim, magnify and thank, the most high supreme and eternal God . . . Creator of all and the Savior . . . lovable, delightful and utterly desirable beyond all else, for ever and ever.[3]

Thomas of Celano, a fellow Franciscan and poet, said of Francis: "He was always occupied with Jesus; Jesus he bore in his heart, Jesus in his mouth, Jesus in his ears, Jesus in his eyes, Jesus in his hands, Jesus in the rest of his members."[4]

Have you ever read the account of a past faith giant and said silently, "I want that—*I really want that*"? That's what I feel when I read accounts of Christ seekers like Francis of Assisi. The apostle Paul captured that same intensity. He summed up his entire reason for being with these words: "That I may know Him and the power of His resurrection and the fellowship of His sufferings, being conformed to His death" (Philippians 3:10 NASB). Take time today, and every day, sitting at the feet of Jesus, basking in His beauty!

A PRAYER FOR TODAY

Beautiful Jesus, I want to spend my life captivated by Your beauty. You are truly beautiful in every way, and Your beauty resonates throughout all creation. Everything about You is beautiful. Everything You do is beautiful. Everything You create is beautiful. Everything You say is beautiful. Today I call to mind specific and personal encounters with Your beauty, that I may meditate on the ways You have revealed Your beauty uniquely to me in the past. I thank You for the beauty with which You have flooded my life; all of it is Yours. May I always truly abound in Your beauty. Amen.

Encountering the *Beautiful* Jesus:
A PRACTICAL APPLICATION

Remember—these four steps, as explained more fully on pages 23–24 in the introduction, are suggested to help you apply this quality of Christ to your own life.

1. **EXPLORE:** Take time to meditate on this quality of Christ. Use Scriptures in this chapter to get started.

2. **EXPERIENCE:** Turn your meditation into prayer that this quality might impact your life today. Pray the above prayer to begin.

3. **EXPRESS:** During your quiet time, take a moment to journal your thoughts, even if briefly.

4. **EXALT:** Pray, praise or even spontaneously sing your way through today's list of the names of Jesus. It only requires a few minutes.

GLORIFY HIS NAME

Therefore I will praise you among the nations,
O LORD; I will sing praises to your *name*.

PSALM 18:49 NIV1984, *emphasis added*

Brightness of His Glory, The
Hebrews 1:3 NKJV

Brilliant Lord Psalm 8:1 MSG

Bringer of Peace Ephesians 2:14 NLT

Builder of Everything Hebrews 3:4 NIV

Capstone, The Psalm 118:22 MSG

Captain of Our Salvation, The
Hebrews 2:10 KJV

Captain of the Host of the Lord
Joshua 5:14 KJV

Castle in Which I Live, The
Psalm 18:1 MSG

Catalyst of a Better Covenant, The
Hebrews 8:6 TPT

Cave to Hide In Psalm 31:5 MSG

Centerpiece of Everything, The
Hebrews 3:4 MSG

Champion Defender Psalm 62:2 TPT

Champion Friend to Widows
Psalm 68:5 TPT

**Champion Who Initiates and
Perfects Our Faith, The**
Hebrews 12:2 NLT

Chief among Ten Thousand
Song of Solomon 5:10 NKJV

Chief Cornerstone, The
Psalm 118:22 NKJV

Chief Foundation Stone, The
1 Peter 2:6 MSG

Chief Shepherd, The 1 Peter 5:4 NKJV

Chosen One, The Luke 23:35 NLT

Christ, the Power of God
1 Corinthians 1:24 NKJV

Christ, Who Is Your Life
Colossians 3:4 NLT

Cliff to Climb Psalm 31:5 MSG

Cloud-Enthroned, The
Revelation 14:14 MSG

Cloud-Rider Psalm 68:4 MSG

Commander Isaiah 55:4 NKJV

Compassionate God
Deuteronomy 4:31 MSG

Compassionate One, The
Isaiah 49:10 MSG

Conclusion, The Revelation 21:6 MSG

Consuming Fire, A Hebrews 12:29 NKJV

**Cornerstone in the Place of Honor,
A** 1 Peter 2:6 MSG

Cornerstone in Zion, A 1 Peter 2:6 TPT

THE
CREATIVE
JESUS

Exploring the Wonders of Christ's Creation

> Christ is the Word who shouted all things into being and who continually calls each of us into fuller being, every day, every minute, right now.
>
> MADELEINE L'ENGLE

FROM THE OUTSET OF OUR STUDY, we have suggested that the characteristic of Christ's supremacy applies to any and all things that might be said of His nature and character. This is certainly true as our Month in the Son brings us into the presence of the *Creative Jesus*. He is, indeed, the Supreme Creator. The apostle John begins his gospel describing the *Creative Jesus*: "He was with God in the beginning. All things were made through him. Nothing that has been made was made without him" (John 1:2–3 NIRV). *The Message* paraphrases these verses thus: "Everything was created through him; nothing—not one thing!—came into being without him." Paul, too, would write of Christ's supremacy over all creation:

> Christ is the visible image of the invisible God. He existed before anything was created and is supreme over all creation, for through

> him God created everything in the heavenly realms and on earth.
> ... Everything was created through him and for him.
>
> COLOSSIANS 1:15–16 NLT

An Atom in the Bucket

Years ago I was fascinated in reading through the Psalms and coming upon a passage that stated: "[The LORD] determines the number of the stars and calls them each by name" (Psalm 147:4 NIV). I paused to think of the ramifications of taking this literally. Of course, there is no reason we should not take it literally. I wondered—if the Lord literally named every star, how many names would be on His list?

To get a grasp of the true significance of the *Creative Jesus*, think of what we presently know about the immensity of the universe. We live in a solar system consisting of one star, the sun, and eight or nine planets, depending on whether you agree with whoever took Pluto off the list or not. Our planet is in a galaxy, the Milky Way, that astronomers say contains at least one hundred billion stars, and each of those could have solar systems as well. By now you realize earth is not only less than a drop in the bucket in the universe, or even a molecule in the bucket; it is barely an atom in the bucket. Indeed, even the Milky Way itself is not much more than an atom in the bucket.

Galaxies come in groups, and these groups have been given names by astronomers. Rather humorously, our galaxy happens to be named the "Local Group"! It includes seventeen galaxies, each also having a minimum of one hundred billion stars (and perhaps many more). Interestingly, the largest known group of galaxies in the universe is called Hercules. It contains an estimated ten thousand separate galaxies. It would require traveling at the speed of light for three hundred million years (that is not a typo) just to reach the first of Hercules's ten thousand galaxies. This vast group, incidentally, is said to contain trillions of stars. (Remember, our solar system has one star!)

Although scientists understandably differ in their conclusions of the ultimate number of galaxies, some have estimates ranging anywhere from ten to forty trillion. That's not stars, or planets, but entire galaxies! The universe is bigger than you think. And Jesus created it all! He created the bucket!

Starstruck

Now comes the interesting exercise. It is estimated there are some forty octillion stars in the known universe. That's the number forty followed by 27 zeros! As I pondered the Lord naming each star, I tried to picture how lengthy a list of forty octillion stars would be. At the time, I pictured a recently purchased (and truly gigantic) *Webster's Unabridged Dictionary* sitting on a shelf near my desk containing nearly five hundred thousand entries. Doing some rudimentary math, I realized it would require eighty quadrillion books the size of Webster's massive unabridged dictionary to list all these stars. (Eighty quadrillion is the number eighty followed by fifteen zeros.)

Now imagine earth covered with some 80,000,000,000 (eighty billion) libraries, each containing one million volumes the size of Webster's huge dictionary. That is what would be required to house those eighty quadrillion books. Further, because these books would be far larger than normal books, each library would require a gigantic multistory building. Picture it this way—imagine every person presently on earth (some 7.7 billion people, including even children) each owning approximately ten of these million-volume libraries, each filled to capacity with a million books the size of Webster's dictionary! The very landscape of planet earth would be covered with nothing but libraries, all containing only the names of stars. Talk about being starstruck!

And Christ, the *Creative Jesus*, was assigned by His Father to speak these stars into existence in the first place. The apostle John certainly did not miss the mark when he concluded his gospel in saying, "Jesus did many other things as well. If every one of them were written down, I suppose that even the whole world would not have room for the books that would be written" (John 21:25 NIV).

And here is an exciting concluding reality—the *Creative Jesus* is only a prayer away from working His creative power in your life today!

A PRAYER FOR TODAY

Jesus, Creator of all things, I step into Your creative presence this very day. You are the Creator who spoke all things into being; You are the Creator who continually breathes life into Your children, sustaining all things. I praise You, Lord, for the wonder of Your creation! I worship You as I stand in amazement of Your creative power. Jesus, I invite Your creative power to work in my own life this day. Create in me a heart that is pleasing to You. Create for me a life that honors You. I submit entirely to Your creative wonder that is at work in my heart this very moment. Amen.

Encountering the *Creative* Jesus:
A PRACTICAL APPLICATION

Remember—these four steps, as explained more fully on pages 23–24 in the introduction, are suggested to help you apply this quality of Christ to your own life.

1. **EXPLORE:** Take time to meditate on this quality of Christ. Use Scriptures in this chapter to get started.

2. **EXPERIENCE:** Turn your meditation into prayer that this quality might impact your life today. Pray the above prayer to begin.

3. **EXPRESS:** During your quiet time, take a moment to journal your thoughts, even if briefly.

4. **EXALT:** Pray, praise or even spontaneously sing your way through today's list of the names of Jesus. It only requires a few minutes.

GLORIFY HIS NAME

Some trust in chariots and some in horses, but
we trust in the *name* of the LORD our God.

PSALM 20:7 NIV, *emphasis added*

Counselor Isaiah 9:6 NKJV

Cover from the Tempest, A
Isaiah 32:2 NKJV

Creator God Psalm 95:6 TPT

Creator of All the Earth, The
Isaiah 40:28 NLT

Creator of All Things
Colossians 1:16 NKJV

Creator of Israel Isaiah 43:15 MSG

Creator of the Heavens Isaiah 42:5 NIV

Crown of Glory, A Isaiah 28:5 NKJV

**David's Spiritual Root and His
Descendant** Revelation 22:16 TPT

Day Star, The 2 Peter 1:19 KJV

Dayspring Light 2 Corinthians 4:4 TPT

**Dazzling Radiance of God's
Splendor, The** Hebrews 1:3 TPT

Deliverer, The Romans 11:26 NKJV

Designer and Builder of All Things
Hebrews 3:4 TPT

Desirable in Every Way
Song of Solomon 5:16 NLT

Devouring Fire, A Hebrews 12:29 NLT

Diadem of Beauty, A Isaiah 28:5 NKJV

Divine Image of God
2 Corinthians 4:4 TPT

Door of the Sheep, The John 10:7 NKJV

Earth-Tamer Psalm 65:7 MSG

Elect One Isaiah 42:1 NKJV

Elect Stone 1 Peter 2:6 NKJV

Emmanuel Matthew 1:23 TPT

Enthroned, The Revelation 21:5 MSG

Eternal Father Isaiah 9:6 MSG

THE
HUMAN
JESUS

Exploring the Wonders of Christ's Humanity

> Jesus was God spelling himself out in language humanity could understand.
>
> S. D. GORDON

N THE CHRISTIAN VIEW, the ultimate evidence for the existence of God is Jesus Christ," wrote Timothy Keller. He adds:

> If there is a God, we characters in his play have to hope that he put some information about himself in the play. But Christians believe he did more than give us information. He wrote himself into the play as the main character in history, when Jesus was born in a manger and rose from the dead.[1]

Theologian James I. Packer adds: "The really staggering Christian claim is that Jesus of Nazareth was God made man. . . . The more you think about it, the more staggering it gets. Nothing in fiction is so fantastic as is this truth of the Incarnation."[2]

Our journey to explore the wonders of the nature and names of Jesus brings us to our view of the *Human Jesus*.

Heaven Meets Earth

The author of Hebrews affirms the significance of the *Human Jesus* throughout his letter. On one occasion he wrote:

> Because God's children are human beings—made of flesh and blood—the Son also became flesh and blood. For only as a human being could he die, and only by dying could he break the power of the devil, who had the power of death. Only in this way could he set free all who have lived their lives as slaves to the fear of dying. . . . Therefore, it was necessary for him to be made in every respect like us, his brothers and sisters, so that he could be our merciful and faithful High Priest before God. Then he could offer a sacrifice that would take away the sins of the people. Since he himself has gone through suffering and testing, he is able to help us when we are being tested.
>
> HEBREWS 2:14–18 NLT

Later in this same letter, more insight is given regarding the profound significance of God taking upon Himself human form in the person of His Son, Jesus Christ:

> You are a priest forever . . . who, in the days of His flesh, when He had offered up prayers and supplications, with vehement cries and tears to Him who was able to save Him from death, and was heard because of His godly fear, though He was a Son, yet He learned obedience by the things which He suffered. And having been perfected, He became the author of eternal salvation to all who obey Him.
>
> HEBREWS 5:6–9 NKJV

Theologians refer to Christ's coming to earth as His incarnation. *Incarnation* is defined as "endowment with a human body; appearance in human form." A simple definition of *human* reads: "having human form or attributes; representative or susceptible to the sympathies and frailties of human nature." The definition expands: "having or sharing qualities viewed as distinctive of people; member of the human race; a living soul; as being a part of humankind." This certainly describes the *Human Jesus*. In referring to Christ as simply the *Word*, the apostle John said of His incarnation: "So the Word became human and made his home among us. He was full of unfailing love and faithfulness. And we have seen his glory, the glory of the Father's one and only Son" (John 1:14 NLT). Henry Law, mid-nineteenth-century Anglican scholar, summed it up in a single sentence: "In Jesus Christ heaven meets earth and earth ascends to heaven."[3]

One of the Sheep

Other Bible writers would likewise speak of the profound significance of Christ's humanity. Paul would tell Colossian believers: "For in Christ lives all the fullness of God in a human body. So you also are complete through your union with Christ, who is the head over every ruler and authority" (Colossians 2:9–10 NLT). Paul would also write to his young colleague Timothy describing Christ's incarnation as a mystery: "Without question, this is the great mystery of our faith: Christ was revealed in a human body and vindicated by the Spirit. He was seen by angels and announced to the nations. He was believed in throughout the world and taken to heaven in glory" (1 Timothy 3:16 NLT).

Of this mystery of Christ's incarnation, Bishop Melito of Sardis in the second century said of Christ:

> He appeared as one of the sheep, yet He still remained the Shepherd. He was esteemed a servant, yet He did not renounce His

Sonship. He was carried in the womb of Mary, yet arrayed in the nature of his Father. He walked upon the earth, yet He filled heaven.[4]

Christianity is clearly unique among all religions in suggesting the very Creator of the universe came to earth in the form of a man to redeem humankind. John Piper asks:

> Does Islam—or any other faith besides Christianity—cherish the crucifixion of the God-Man, Jesus Christ, as the only ground of our acceptance with God? The answer is no. Only Christians "follow the Lamb" who was "slain" as the one and only Redeemer who sits on the "throne" of God (Revelation 14:4; 5:6; 7:17). . . . The closer you get to what makes Christianity ghastly, the closer you get to what makes it glorious.[5]

Are you ready to get closer? Let's continue our journey. There is so much more to come!

A PRAYER FOR TODAY

Jesus, today I come before You to thank You for taking on flesh and blood and walking this earth as one of us. Only in human form could You die and conquer the power of death. Only in a human body could You bear the sufferings of humankind and share their pain. Only in a human body could You truly be "God with us." As I focus today on Your humanity, I become aware of how deeply I am able to trust You. You truly know, understand and sympathetically share in my humanness. Thank You for Your nearness, Lord Jesus. Amen.

Encountering the *Human* Jesus:
A PRACTICAL APPLICATION

Remember—these four steps, as explained more fully on pages 23–24 in the introduction, are suggested to help you apply this quality of Christ to your own life.

1. **EXPLORE:** Take time to meditate on this quality of Christ. Use Scriptures in this chapter to get started.

2. **EXPERIENCE:** Turn your meditation into prayer that this quality might impact your life today. Pray the above prayer to begin.

3. **EXPRESS:** During your quiet time, take a moment to journal your thoughts, even if briefly.

4. **EXALT:** Pray, praise or even spontaneously sing your way through today's list of the names of Jesus. It only requires a few minutes.

GLORIFY HIS NAME

Ascribe to the LORD the glory due his *name*; worship
the LORD in the splendor of his holiness.

PSALM 29:2 NIV, *emphasis added*

Eternal King, The Jeremiah 10:10 MSG

Eternal Life 1 John 5:20 NLT, NKJV

Eternal Life-Giver 1 John 1:2 TPT

Eternally Blessed God, The
Romans 9:5 NKJV

Ever and Always Psalm 45:6 MSG

Everlasting Father Isaiah 9:6 NKJV

Everlasting King Jeremiah 10:10 NKJV

Exact Likeness of God, The
2 Corinthians 4:4 NLT

Exalted God, The 1 Timothy 6:15 TPT

Faithful and True Witness, The
Revelation 3:14 NLT

Faithful God, A Deuteronomy 32:4 NLT

Father of Compassion
2 Corinthians 1:3 NIV

Father of Mercies, The
2 Corinthians 1:3 NKJV

Father of Orphans Psalm 68:5 MSG

Fearsome Job 25:2 MSG

Finisher of Our Faith Hebrews 12:2 NKJV

**First and Last and Everything in
Between** Isaiah 44:6 MSG

**Firstborn among Many Brethren,
The** Romans 8:29 NKJV

Firstborn from the Dead, The
Colossians 1:18 NKJV

Firstborn Heir in Resurrection
Colossians 1:18 TPT

Firstborn over All Creation, The
Colossians 1:15 NKJV

**Firstfruits of Those Who
Have Fallen Asleep, The**
1 Corinthians 15:20 NKJV

First of God's Creation
Revelation 3:14 MSG

First on the Scene Isaiah 41:4 MSG

Flame, A Isaiah 10:17 NLT

Focus of My Delight Matthew 17:5 MSG

Forerunner, The Hebrews 6:20 NKJV

Forever Exalted Psalm 92:8 NIV

Forgiving Redeemer 1 John 2:1 TPT

THE
DIVINE
JESUS

Exploring the Wonders of Christ's Divinity

> Two thousand years ago there was One here on this earth who
> lived the grandest life that ever has been lived yet—a life that
> every thinking man, with deeper or shallower meaning, has
> agreed to call divine.
>
> FREDERICK W. ROBERTSON

WHILE RECOGNIZING THAT CHRIST was indeed human, and fully so, we must likewise recognize that He was and is fully God as well. Novatian, a Roman theologian and scholar (c. 235), said of Christ: "He is indeed proved to be the Son of His Father. But He is found to be both Lord and God of all else. . . . For He is God, and all things are subjected to Him."[1] Almost a century after Novatian wrote these words, the framers of the Nicene Creed (AD 325) would declare, "Christ is One Lord, only begotten Son of God; begotten of the Father before all worlds; God of God, Light of Light, very God of very God." This brings our journey of a Month in the Son to explore the wonders of the *Divine Jesus.*

Most readers would have a basic understanding of the meaning of *divine,* but allow me to expand on it a bit. A more complete definition of *divine* reads: "That which suggests the nature of, or is associated with or derived from God; connotes supreme greatness; belonging to or coming from God; Almighty, Author, Creator, Supreme Being." Also: "Of, relating to, or proceeding directly from God; being a deity (i.e., the divine Savior)."

Dazzling Radiance

The apostle Paul was clear in his writings that although Christ was human, He was fully divine. In his second letter to the Corinthian believers, he wrote: "At one time we thought of Christ merely from a human point of view. How differently we know him now! This means that anyone who belongs to Christ has become a new person. The old life is gone; a new life has begun!" (2 Corinthians 5:16–17 NLT). Paul then highlights his clear understanding of the deity of Christ:

> And all of this is a gift from God, who brought us back to himself through Christ. And God has given us this task of reconciling people to him. For God was in Christ, reconciling the world to himself, no longer counting people's sins against them. And he gave us this wonderful message of reconciliation.
>
> 2 CORINTHIANS 5:18–19 NLT

Here we especially note Paul's explanation that "God was in Christ, reconciling the world to himself." To believers in Rome, Paul would directly claim Jesus to be God: "Christ himself was an Israelite as far as his human nature is concerned. *And he is God*, the one who rules over everything and is worthy of eternal praise! Amen" (Romans 9:5 NLT, emphasis added). Paul would likewise write Titus: "We should live in this evil world with wisdom, righteousness, and devotion to God, while we look forward with hope to that wonderful day when the glory of *our great God and Savior, Jesus Christ,* will be revealed" (Titus 2:12b–13 NLT, emphasis added).

Peter also can be added to our list of those apostles who referenced Christ as God and Savior: "I am writing to you who share the same precious faith we have. This faith was given to you because of the justice and fairness of *Jesus Christ, our God and Savior*" (2 Peter 1:1 NLT, emphasis added).

The author of Hebrews likewise adds his voice in declaring Christ as fully divine when writing: "The Son is the dazzling radiance of God's splendor, the exact expression of God's true nature—his mirror image! He holds the universe together and expands it by the mighty power of his spoken word" (Hebrews 1:3 TPT). Christ is indeed God. I agree with John Piper: "God without Christ is no God. . . . God-in-Christ is the only true God and the only path to joy. . . . If we would see and savor the glory of God, we must see and savor Christ."[2]

The Bottom Line

Of importance to note is that Christ Himself declared He was God. He told harassing Jewish authorities, "Most assuredly, I say to you, the Son can do nothing of Himself, but what He sees the Father do; for whatever He does, the Son also does in like manner" (John 5:19 NKJV). Later, when speaking with the Pharisees, Christ described His disciples as sheep who follow Him and even boldly declared that He gave them eternal life and that they would never perish (John 10:27–28 NKJV). Jesus further highlighted His deity in saying, "I and My Father are one" (verse 30 NKJV).

One of history's oft-repeated fallacies comes from those who say Christ was merely a great human being, a wonderful moral teacher and even a prophet, but not divine. C. S. Lewis addressed this fallacy in his classic work *Mere Christianity*:

> A man who was merely a man and said the sort of things Jesus said would not be a great moral teacher. He would either be a lunatic—on a level with the man who says he is a poached egg—or else he would be the devil of hell. You must make your choice. Either this man was, and is, the Son of God, or else a madman or something worse. You can shut him up for a fool, you can spit at him and kill him as a demon or you can fall at his feet and call him Lord and God.[3]

May we choose this day, and every day, to fall at the feet of our Lord and God—the *Divine Jesus*!

A PRAYER FOR TODAY

Jesus—divine lord, divine Savior, one true God—I bow before You today as I gaze upon Your divine glory. You alone are God and divine Lord of the universe. I submit all my life to You, knowing that You hold me close to your heart. Your ways are perfect. You are fully God and the sovereign heavenly King. Thank You, God, for reconciling us to Yourself through Jesus. Thank You for coming into our world that we might encounter You in Your divine majesty. I invite You to be entirely divine in my own life today—and make me ever more like You. Amen.

Encountering the *Divine* Jesus:
A PRACTICAL APPLICATION

Remember—these four steps, as explained more fully on pages 23–24 in the introduction, are suggested to help you apply this quality of Christ to your own life.

1. **EXPLORE:** Take time to meditate on this quality of Christ. Use Scriptures in this chapter to get started.

2. **EXPERIENCE:** Turn your meditation into prayer that this quality might impact your life today. Pray the above prayer to begin.

3. **EXPRESS:** During your quiet time, take a moment to journal your thoughts, even if briefly.

4. **EXALT:** Pray, praise or even spontaneously sing your way through today's list of the names of Jesus. It only requires a few minutes.

GLORIFY HIS NAME

I will give thanks to the LORD because of his righteousness
and will sing praise to the *name* of the LORD Most High.

PSALM 7:17 NIV1984, *emphasis added*

Fortified Tower, A Proverbs 18:10 NIV

Fortress Psalm 18:2 NLT

Foundation, A Isaiah 28:16 NKJV

Foundation in Zion, A Isaiah 28:16 MSG

Fountain of Cascading Light, A
Psalm 36:9 MSG

Fountain of Fresh Flowing Waters,
The Jeremiah 2:13 MSG

Fountain of Life Psalm 36:9 NIV

Fountain of Living Water, The
Jeremiah 17:13 NLT

Fragrant Offering, A Ephesians 5:2 NIV

Friend Who Sticks Closer Than a
Brother, A Proverbs 18:24 NKJV

Garden of Renown, A
Ezekiel 34:29 NKJV

Gate, The John 10:1-2 MSG

Generous in Love Psalm 100:5 MSG

Gift God Has for You, The
John 4:10 NLT

Giver of Great Victory
2 Samuel 22:51 NLT

Glorious Crown Isaiah 28:5 NLT

Glorious God Acts 7:2 NLT

Glorious Lord, The Isaiah 33:21 KJV

Glorious Throne to His Father's
House, A Isaiah 22:23 NKJV

Glory-Fortress Psalm 59:16 TPT

Glory of Your People Israel, The
Luke 2:32 NLT

God about to Arrive, The
Revelation 1:4 MSG

God and Master of the Spirits
of the Prophets, The
Revelation 22:6 MSG

God Awesome Isaiah 35:2 MSG

God-Enthroned Revelation 21:5 TPT

God Full of Compassion, A
Psalm 86:15 NKJV

God Immense and Powerful and
Awesome Deuteronomy 10:17 MSG

THE
OBEDIENT
JESUS

Exploring the Wonders
of Christ's Obedience

As a skilled master teaches both by example and command, so Christ taught obedience, even to the point of death, by dying to Himself in obedience.

RUFINIUS OF CONCORDIA (AD 411–345)

I N OUR JOURNEY THUS FAR, we have looked at various aspects of Christ's awesome nature and character and viewed them through the lens of His supremacy. We come now to view our Savior through the prism of His supreme obedience. He is the *Obedient Jesus*. When thinking of the unity within the Trinity and what that harmonious existence must have involved, it is difficult to imagine what it must have been like for Christ to leave the splendor of His heavenly existence when He became one of us. It becomes clear from the outset that obedience was the beginning point of Christ's incarnation. He was willing to submit to His heavenly Father in order to offer Himself as the supreme sacrifice for the sins of humankind.

A Willingness to Submit

Obedience by definition is "the willingness to submit to one in author-ity or control; to be guided by or willing to submit to the orders of one who is superior." We see Christ freely and willingly responding in total obedience to all that His heavenly Father asked Him to do. Paul began his letter to the Galatian believers saying, "Grace and peace to you from God our Father and the Lord Jesus Christ, who gave himself for our sins to rescue us from the present evil age, according to the will of our God and Father, to whom be glory for ever and ever. Amen" (Galatians 1:3–5 NIV).

Christ's primary goal was always to do the will of the Father, which requires obedience. If there were no obedience, there would be no cross. If there were no cross, there would be no resurrection. Obedience thus becomes fundamentally essential for Christ to fulfill His earthly mis-sion. Henry Blackaby, who impacted millions with his teaching on *Expe-riencing God*, wrote: "Jesus knew God's will, and in prayer He submitted Himself to it. He arose from His knees at Gethsemane and followed the Father to the cross."[1]

Master of All

We see other examples of Christ's obedience in Scripture. On one oc-casion, His disciples encouraged Him to have something to eat. He responded: "I have food to eat that you know nothing about" (John 4:32 NIV). The disciples were confused by this response, and Jesus added: "My food . . . is to do the will of him who sent me and to finish his work" (John 4:34 NIV). Again, we see the obedience of Christ in His response. Of this passage, John Piper wrote: "Jesus cherished his Father's will like we cherish food. To finish his Father's work was what he fed upon; to abandon it would be to choose starvation."[2]

We also see the submissive quality of Christ's obedience when He spoke of Himself as the "bread of life" (John 6:35 NIV). He explains, "All those the Father gives me will come to me, and whoever comes to me I will never drive away. For I have come down from heaven not to do my will but to do the will of him who sent me" (John 6:37–38 NIV).

Paul's writings also call attention to the obedience of Christ. He writes:

> Yes, Adam's one sin brings condemnation for everyone, but Christ's one act of righteousness brings a right relationship with God and new life for everyone. Because one person disobeyed God, many became sinners. But because one other person obeyed God, many will be made righteous.
>
> ROMANS 5:18–19 NLT

To believers at Philippi, Paul would explain that it was through Christ's obedience that God exalted His Son to the highest place of honor in the universe. We read:

> Because of [Christ's] obedience, God lifted him high and honored him far beyond anyone or anything, ever, so that all created beings in heaven and on earth—even those long ago dead and buried—will bow in worship before this Jesus Christ, and call out in praise that he is the Master of all, to the glorious honor of God the Father.
>
> PHILIPPIANS 2:9–11 MSG

The Step of Yes

The importance of obedience in the life of Christ is also uniquely high-lighted by the author of Hebrews. He wrote:

> God had the power to save Jesus from death. And while Jesus was on earth, he begged God with loud crying and tears to save him. He truly worshiped God, and God listened to his prayers. Jesus is God's own Son, but still he had to suffer before he could learn what it really means to obey God. Suffering made Jesus perfect, and now he can save forever all who obey him.
>
> HEBREWS 5:7–9 CEV

To walk daily alongside the *Obedient Jesus* is to walk in a lifestyle of day-by-day obedience. It is always the first step in the direction of fulfilling God's will for our lives. What has so marked the lives of God's giants of faith throughout history has been their almost radical willingness to live an unconditional lifestyle of obedience. In his classic book *God's Smuggler*, Brother Andrew described his calling to just such a lifestyle that would take him many times behind the Iron Curtain smuggling Bibles to spiritually starving believers. It began with this determined prayer of obedience:

> Whenever, wherever, however You want me, I'll go. And I'll begin this very minute. Lord, as I stand up from this place, and as I take my first step forward, will You consider this is a step toward complete obedience to You? I'll call it the step of yes.[3]

As we continue our journey in exploring the wonders of Christ's nature and names, may each step we take be a step of yes!

A PRAYER FOR TODAY

Jesus, I bring my attention to Your obedience today. I honor the submission You willingly chose in all things. I am deeply grateful for Your obedience to the cross. Lord, I long to be like You. I see the fruit of Your obedience—the seamless intimacy You share with the Father—and I want to pattern my life after Yours for the sake of that same intimacy. Lead me in obedience, Jesus. Make my heart sensitive to Your voice that I might always know how to walk in Your ways. Today, oh Lord, I take the step of yes! Amen.

Encountering the *Obedient* Jesus:
A PRACTICAL APPLICATION

Remember—these four steps, as explained more fully on pages 23–24 in the introduction, are suggested to help you apply this quality of Christ to your own life.

1. **EXPLORE:** Take time to meditate on this quality of Christ. Use Scriptures in this chapter to get started.

2. **EXPERIENCE:** Turn your meditation into prayer that this quality might impact your life today. Pray the above prayer to begin.

3. **EXPRESS:** During your quiet time, take a moment to journal your thoughts, even if briefly.

4. **EXALT:** Pray, praise or even spontaneously sing your way through today's list of the names of Jesus. It only requires a few minutes.

GLORIFY HIS NAME

Lord, our Lord, how majestic is your *name* in all the
earth! You have set your glory above the heavens.

PSALM 8:1 NIV1984, *emphasis added*

God Is Judge Hebrews 12:23 MSG

God Is My Strength and Power
2 Samuel 22:33 NKJV

God Is Powerful and Dreadful
Job 25:2 NLT

God Majestic Isaiah 33:21 MSG

God My Dependable Love
Psalm 59:17 MSG

God My Savior Luke 1:47 NKJV

God Near at Hand, A
Jeremiah 23:23 MSG

God Nearby Jeremiah 23:23 NIV

God of All Comfort
2 Corinthians 1:3 NKJV

God of All Gods, The Daniel 2:47 MSG

God of All Grace, The 1 Peter 5:10 NKJV

God of All Healing Counsel
2 Corinthians 1:3 MSG

God of Bethel, The Genesis 31:13 MSG

God of Compassion and Mercy, A
Psalm 86:15 NLT

God of Everything Living, The
Jeremiah 32:26 MSG

God of Faithfulness Psalm 31:5 TPT

God of Glory, The Acts 7:2 NKJV

God of Great Wonders Psalm 77:14 NLT

God of Hope, The Romans 15:13 NKJV

God of Israel, The Psalm 59:5 NKJV

God of Love and Peace, The
2 Corinthians 13:11 NLT

God of My Ecstatic Joy Psalm 43:4 TPT

God of Passionate Love
Psalm 59:10 TPT

God of Patience and Comfort, The
Romans 15:5 NKJV

God of Recompense, The
Jeremiah 51:56 NKJV

God of Salvation Psalm 68:20 NKJV

God-of-the-Angel-Armies
Psalm 24:10 MSG

God of the Highest Place
Psalm 7:17 TPT

THE
SUFFERING
JESUS

Exploring the Wonders of Christ's Sacrifice

> O, precious blood of my Redeemer, O, gaping wounds of my cru-
> cified Savior. Who can contemplate the sufferings of God incar-
> nate, and not raise his hope, and not put his trust in Him?
>
> RICHARD ALLEN (C. 1815)

TO UNDERSTAND THE IMMENSITY of the impact of
Christ's life, we must go back to the foot of the cross. Just as
no other major religion in the world claims a Savior who was
God who came from the heavens to live among men, no other religion
has a cross. The cross is the epitome of suffering. It is at the cross we
come to understand suffering to the extreme. It is here we meet the
Suffering Jesus and come to understand the supreme sacrifice made
for the redemption of humankind.

The cross is clearly the preeminent picture of the sacrifice of one for
the sake of another, which is a primary definition of the word *sacrifice*.
Soldiers in our wars who intentionally fall on a live grenade to save
other soldiers are called heroes and often are awarded the treasured
Congressional Medal of Honor posthumously for their heroism. At Cal-
vary, Christ fell upon the sins of all of humanity so that any who would
believe in Him would have eternal life.

Eugene H. Peterson, best known for his widely received paraphrase of Scripture, *The Message*, said of the cross:

> The single, overwhelming fact of history is the crucifixion of Jesus Christ. There is no military battle, no geographical exploration, no scientific discovery, no literary creation, no artistic achievement, no moral heroism that compares with it. It is unique, massive, monumental, unprecedented, and unparalleled. . . . The cross of Christ is the central fact to which all other facts are subordinate.[1]

Destined for the Cross

The word *suffer* means: "To undergo something painful or unpleasant, as injury, grief or loss." It also is, "To feel keenly; to labor under stress; to undergo a process of pain or to feel deep sadness or mental pain." Interestingly, our word *suffer* comes from the Latin word *sufferer*, meaning "to submit to; to endure." It is derived from the Latin words *sub* and *ferre* meaning "to carry; or to bear." The cross is clearly a one-word summary of the totality of the meaning of suffering.

Of all the apostles, Peter spoke often of the sufferings of Christ, especially as to the suffering that relates to those who follow our Lord. Peter wrote, "For God called you to do good, even if it means suffering, just as Christ suffered for you. He is your example, and you must follow in his steps" (1 Peter 2:21 NLT). In that same chapter, the apostle added, "[Christ] personally carried our sins in his body on the cross so that we can be dead to sin and live for what is right. By his wounds you are healed" (1 Peter 2:24 NLT).

Jesus knew well He was destined for the cross. In referring to that destiny, Christ said,

> "I am the good shepherd. The good shepherd lays down his life for the sheep. . . . The reason my Father loves me is that I lay down my life—only to take it up again. No one takes it from me, but I lay it down of my own accord. I have authority to lay it down and authority to take it up again. This command I received from my Father."
>
> JOHN 10:11, 17–18 NIV

Of this discourse recorded by John, Matthew Henry, in referencing the sacrificing of sheep in the ancient Jewish tradition, wrote in his commentary, "Thousands of sheep had been offered in sacrifice for their shepherds, as sin-offerings, but here, by a surprising reverse, the shepherd is sacrificed for the sheep."[2]

God's Megaphone

Although the cross was a picture of supreme suffering, it also was a picture of supreme triumph. Paul, in mentioning Christ's sufferings, spoke of this triumph to his young colleague Timothy: "If we are joined with him in his sufferings, then we will reign together with him in his triumph" (2 Timothy 2:12 TPT). Paul Billheimer, a man I greatly admired, wrote a classic book titled *Don't Waste Your Sorrows*. Billheimer believed that the believer's sufferings were often tools the Lord used to equip and perfect them. C. S. Lewis agreed: "Pain removes the veil; it plants the flag of truth within the fortress of a rebel soul."[3] Archbishop Fulton J. Sheen likewise agreed. He believed suffering sometimes prepares those who suffer with a special sensitivity to hear the voice of the Lord. With the picture of Christ's nail-scarred hands in his mind, Sheen wrote: "Pain is God's megaphone. Show me your hands. Do they bear the scars of suffering?"

Dear reader, don't waste your sorrows. Glory in the cross. If pain is in your present, triumph is in your future. John Piper wisely advises, "Life is wasted if we do not grasp the glory of the cross, cherish it for the treasure that it is, and cleave to it as the highest price of every pleasure and the deepest comfort in every pain."[4]

As our Month in the Son comes this day to a more painful view of our supreme Jesus, may we remember that to walk daily beside the *Suffering Jesus* is to express our willingness to bear whatever personal cross we must bear in order to be like Him. In the end, we are certain, our cross also will lead to both glory and triumph!

A PRAYER FOR TODAY

Jesus, it is by Your suffering that I have salvation. As I spend time in Your presence today, I linger at the foot of the cross. I look upon Your head and Your hands and Your feet. I notice every wound and know that each was received on my behalf. I think also of Your personal sufferings prior to the cross—each day as You walked the earth among us, intimately knowing the excruciating sorrows of broken humankind. Every pain of life and death You bore for me, Jesus. You are truly worthy to receive the reward of Your suffering. Amen.

Encountering the *Suffering* Jesus:
A PRACTICAL APPLICATION

Remember—these four steps, as explained more fully on pages 23–24 in the introduction, are suggested to help you apply this quality of Christ to your own life.

1. **EXPLORE:** Take time to meditate on this quality of Christ. Use Scriptures in this chapter to get started.

2. **EXPERIENCE:** Turn your meditation into prayer that this quality might impact your life today. Pray the above prayer to begin.

3. **EXPRESS:** During your quiet time, take a moment to journal your thoughts, even if briefly.

4. **EXALT:** Pray, praise or even spontaneously sing your way through today's list of the names of Jesus. It only requires a few minutes.

GLORIFY HIS NAME

Since you are my rock and my fortress, for the
sake of your *name* lead and guide me.

PSALM 31:3 NIV, *emphasis added*

God of the Whole Earth, The
Isaiah 54:5 NKJV

God of Truth, A Deuteronomy 32:4 NKJV

God of Zion Psalm 110:2 MSG

God Our Savior Psalm 68:19 NLT

God's Gracious Gift Romans 5:15 NLT

God's Messenger Hebrews 3:1 NLT

God's Passover Lamb John 1:29 MSG

God the Judge of All
Hebrews 12:23 NKJV

God the Source of Great Endurance
and Comfort Romans 15:5 TPT

God Who Alone Is Wise
1 Timothy 1:17 NKJV

God Who Armed Me Well, The
2 Samuel 22:33 MSG

God Who Builds a Road Right
through the Ocean, The
Isaiah 43:16 MSG

God Who Created the Cosmos,
The Isaiah 42:5 MSG

God Who Does What He Says, A
Isaiah 31:2 MSG

God Who Does Wonders
Psalm 77:14 NKJV

God Who Formed You in the
Womb Isaiah 44:2 MSG

God Who Gives Just Punishment
Jeremiah 51:56 NLT

God Who Gives Me Life Psalm 42:8 NLT

God Who Gives Us His Peace and
Wholeness Romans 15:33 TPT

God Who Inspires the Prophets
Revelation 22:6 NIV

God Who Knows What He's Doing
Isaiah 31:2 MSG

God Who Makes Things Happen,
The Psalm 77:14 MSG

God Who Performs Miracles
Psalm 77:14 NIV

God-Who-Puts-Everything-Right
Jeremiah 23:6 MSG

God Who Saved You, The
Hosea 13:4 MSG

God-Who-Saves-Us Psalm 68:19 MSG

God Who Sees Me, The
Genesis 16:13 MSG

God Who Shows Me Unfailing Love
Psalm 59:17 NLT

THE
RESURRECTED
JESUS

Exploring the Wonders
of Christ's Resurrection

The Resurrection lights that darkest area of life—death—and lights it, not with a verbal word of encouragement, but with a vital word of incarnate victory: He arose! That is the most luminous fact of history.

E. STANLEY JONES

RESURRECTION MORNING! Imagine for a moment what that monumental event must have been like! Passion plays of all sorts across the world on Easter Sunday seek to portray it. With modern technology, some have flashing strobes, manufactured lightning accompanied by blazing acoustical thunderclaps with other pyrotechnics designed to somehow portray this extraordinary defining moment in history. Centuries ago, Hilary of Poitiers, who was Bishop of Poitiers during her lifetime (AD 310–367), gave his memorable review:

> The earth shook. For the earth could not hold this dead man. Rocks were split, for the Word of God and the power of his eternal goodness rushed in, penetrating every stronghold and principality. Graves were opened, for the gates of death had been unlocked. And a number of the bodies of the saints who had fallen asleep arose.

> Dispelling the shadows of death and illuminating the darkness of hell, Christ destroyed the spoils of death itself at the resurrection of the saints, who saw him immediately.[1]

Indisputable

With these introductory thoughts, our Month in the Son brings us to the feet of the *Resurrected Jesus*. The resurrection was clearly a theme wherever the apostle Paul preached during his missionary journeys. When arriving in Antioch, Paul and his team went to the synagogue on the Sabbath and sat down to listen to Jewish leaders read from the Law and the Prophets. The leaders recognizing these guests among them invited them to address the gathering. Paul immediately seized this opportunity and began to teach something of a history lesson of the Jewish people from the time of the Exodus to the crucifixion and resurrection of Christ. He explained how the prophets had foretold the coming Messiah. He argued that the resurrection of Christ was indisputable. Describing the moments that led up to the crucifixion, and the resurrection that followed, Paul declared:

> After they [Jewish authorities] had done everything the prophets said they would do, they took him down from the cross and buried him. And then God raised him from death. There is no disputing that—he appeared over and over again many times and places to those who had known him well in the Galilean years, and these same people continue to give witness that he is alive.
>
> Acts 13:29b–31 msg

Paul would likewise highlight the importance of the resurrection when he wrote to Roman believers:

> Now if we died with Christ, we believe that we shall also live with Him, knowing that Christ, being raised from the dead, will never die again; death has no further dominion over Him. For the death He died, He died to sin once for all, but the life He lives, He lives to God.
>
> ROMANS 6:8–10 MEV

Of course, Jesus Himself not only prophesied His resurrection, He promised His disciples they, too, would experience it. John records these words of Christ: "I am, right now, Resurrection and Life. The one who believes in me, even though he or she dies, will live. And everyone who lives believing in me does not ultimately die at all. Do you believe this?" (John 11:25–26 MSG).

The Future Starts Now

Christ's resurrection is, indeed, glorious news, and it makes the Good News really, really good! The apostle Peter celebrated this when he wrote:

> What a God we have! And how fortunate we are to have him, this Father of our Master Jesus! Because Jesus was raised from the dead, we've been given a brand-new life and have everything to live for, including a future in heaven—and the future starts now!
>
> 1 PETER 1:3–4 MSG

This affirms that followers of Christ are already living resurrected lives. We simply need to believe it and live it! The profound sufferings of Christ on the cross as He wore a painful crown of thorns were transformed in an instant three days later at His resurrection. In that moment, a new crown replaced the old—a crown of kingly glory. A. W. Tozer said, "We understand and acknowledge that the Resurrection has placed a glorious crown upon all of Christ's sufferings."[2]

David Bryant, whom I cite often in these pages, provides this powerful summary to the resurrection's significance:

> Christianity is the only religion in the world that depends on a miracle for . . . its reason to exist. Other faiths may acknowledge miracles, but the Christian movement stands or falls based on the historicity of one grand miracle—which also happens to be one of the greatest miracles ever! Among spiritual founders, prophets, and leaders of world religions, the resurrection of our Founder and Leader remains unprecedented, lifting Christ beyond all competitors and contenders for the throne of the universe.[3]
>
> Christ the Lord is risen today, Alleluia!
> Sons of men and angels say, Alleluia!
> Raise your joys and triumphs high, Alleluia!
> Sing, ye heavens, and earth, reply, Alleluia![4]
>
> —CHARLES WESLEY (1707-1788)

A PRAYER FOR TODAY

Jesus, I celebrate Your resurrection today! I worship You, the Risen One. I sing the praises of Your triumph over death and proclaim my faith in Your resurrected life. Sanctify my imagination as I read Your Word, Lord, and as I step into the story of Your resurrection. Allow me to feel the shock and wonder of Your appearance outside the grave. May my heart catch a glimpse of the freedom Your disciples felt—the transformation of their fear into boldness. I want to be utterly changed by Your resurrection, Jesus. I invite Your resurrection life to live inside of me today. Amen.

Encountering the *Resurrected* Jesus:
A PRACTICAL APPLICATION

Remember—these four steps, as explained more fully on pages 23–24 in the introduction, are suggested to help you apply this quality of Christ to your own life.

1. **EXPLORE:** Take time to meditate on this quality of Christ. Use Scriptures in this chapter to get started.

2. **EXPERIENCE:** Turn your meditation into prayer that this quality might impact your life today. Pray the above prayer to begin.

3. **EXPRESS:** During your quiet time, take a moment to journal your thoughts, even if briefly.

4. **EXALT:** Pray, praise or even spontaneously sing your way through today's list of the names of Jesus. It only requires a few minutes.

GLORIFY HIS NAME

Glorify the LORD with me; let us exalt his *name* together.

PSALM 34:3 NIV, *emphasis added*

God Who Was, The Revelation 1:4 MSG

God Who Works Behind the
Scenes, A Isaiah 45:15 MSG

God Who Works in Mysterious
Ways Isaiah 45:15 NLT

God with Us Matthew 1:23 NKJV

God-Wrapped-around-Us as Our
Shield Psalm 115:11 TPT

God You Can Depend Upon, A
Deuteronomy 7:9 MSG

God-Your-Salvation Isaiah 17:10 MSG

Good Place to Hide Psalm 59:16 MSG

Greatest of All Psalm 95:3 TPT

Guarantor of a Better Covenant,
The Hebrews 7:22 NIV

Guardian-God for His People,
Israel Psalm 121:4 TPT

Guardian of Your Souls 1 Peter 2:25 NLT

Guest Room Where I Can Retreat,
A Psalm 71:3 MSG

Habitation of Justice, The
Jeremiah 50:7 NKJV

Head of Every Man, The
1 Corinthians 11:3 NLT

Head of the Body, The
Colossians 1:18 NKJV

Head of the Church Colossians 1:18 NLT

Head of the House Luke 13:25 TPT

Head over All Things Ephesians 1:22 NLT

Healing Ointments in Gilead
Jeremiah 8:22 MSG

Heaven-High God Psalm 7:17 MSG

Heaven-Throned God Psalm 2:4 MSG

Heir of All Things Hebrews 1:2 NKJV

Help and Shield Psalm 115:9–11 NIV

Helper Psalm 115:9–11 MSG

Help of My Countenance, The
Psalm 42:11 NKJV

He Who Lives Revelation 1:18 NKJV

He Who Is Coming Hebrews 10:37 NKJV

THE
ASCENDED
JESUS

Exploring the Wonders of Christ's Ascension

> Christ was taken up into heaven, not to enjoy blessed rest at a distance from us, but to govern the world for the salvation of all believers.
>
> JOHN CALVIN

N WRITING HIS CLASSIC STUDY OF CHRISTOLOGY, *Christ Is Now*, David Bryant asks a compelling question:

> Of the rich spectrum of biblical doctrines underpinning the historic Christian faith, which truth do you think may be the most widely neglected teaching within the contemporary Church—particularly among nearly three-quarters of a billion Christians who make up the global evangelical movement?[1]

Bryant then expands that question and provides a personal answer:

> Could it be the Trinity? The Atonement? The Second Coming? The role of miracles? Moral purity? Actually, across the Body of Christ, believers are regularly exposed to all of these topics, Sunday after Sunday. But something crucial is missing. What is it? Here's my answer: It's the doctrine of the Ascension![2]

These moments in our Month in the Son seek to address that issue as we come to know more intimately the *Ascended Jesus*.

A Christ-Saturated Universe

Paul, in his letter to Ephesian believers, highlighted the significance of Christ's ascension as he describes his heartfelt apostolic prayers on their behalf:

> Ever since I first heard of your strong faith in the Lord Jesus and your love for God's people everywhere, I have not stopped thanking God for you. . . . I also pray that you will understand the incredible greatness of God's power for us who believe him. This is the same mighty power that raised Christ from the dead and seated him in the place of honor at God's right hand in the heavenly realms. Now he is far above any ruler or authority or power or leader or anything else—not only in this world but also in the world to come.
>
> Ephesians 1:15–16a, 19–21 nlt

Later in the same letter, Paul would tell these believers that Christ "ascended higher than all the heavens, so that he might fill the entire universe with himself" (Ephesians 4:10 nlt). Try to imagine the full meaning of a Christ-saturated universe. The simple phrase "so that he might fill the entire universe with himself" brings us back to the significance of the supremacy of Christ in all things.

Indeed, as I suggested at the very outset of our journey, one must generously use the word *supreme* in looking at any aspects of Christ's nature and character. He is supreme in His beauty, supreme in His role as Creator, clearly supreme in His resurrection and even supreme in His suffering. He is likewise supreme in His ascension. Bear in mind the word *supreme* means: "most excellent; highest in rank, power and authority; utmost; ultimate; superior." Supreme is almost synonymous with Christ's ascension.

Paul would also highlight Christ's exalted supremacy when he spoke to Philippian believers regarding Christ's ascension:

> Who [Christ], being in very nature God, did not consider equality with God something to be used to his own advantage; rather, he made himself nothing by taking the very nature of a servant, being made in human likeness. . . . Therefore God exalted him to the highest place and gave him the name that is above every name.
>
> PHILIPPIANS 2:6–9 NIV

History's Defining Moment

We further see this theme sprinkled throughout Scripture whenever there is a reference to the Lord being exalted. The psalmist declared: "The LORD reigns, let the peoples tremble; He is enthroned above the cherubim, let the earth shake! The LORD is great in Zion, and He is exalted above all the peoples. Let them praise Your great and awesome name; Holy is He" (Psalm 99:1–3 NASB). Elsewhere he wrote, "For you, O LORD, are supreme over all the earth; you are exalted far above all gods" (Psalm 97:9 NLT).

All of these promises and declarations find their ultimate expression in the ascension of Jesus Christ. It was, quite simply, history's defining moment. Even Jesus Himself, speaking in the third person, said:

> "If I told you earthly things and you do not believe, how will you believe if I tell you heavenly things? No one has ascended into heaven, but He who descended from heaven: the Son of Man. As Moses lifted up the serpent in the wilderness, even so must the Son

of Man be lifted up; so that whoever believes will in Him have eternal life."

JOHN 3:12–15 NASB

Luke's account of the ascension, also described in Acts 1:9–11, reads:

Then Jesus led them to Bethany, and lifting his hands to heaven, he blessed them. While he was blessing them, he left them and was taken up to heaven. So they worshiped him and then returned to Jerusalem filled with great joy. And they spent all of their time in the Temple, praising God.

LUKE 24:50–53 NLT

Of this culminating moment in the life of Christ's earthly journey, David Bryant concludes:

That one historical event, in time and space and history, carried with it eternal consequences that the redeemed will never cease recounting in sheer amazement. Jesus ascended! All royal enthronements of history combined could never excel that one. It is the preeminent imperial investiture of all time.

A PRAYER FOR TODAY

Jesus, high and exalted! *Jesus, the One who fills the earth with righteousness and justice! Jesus, You reign on high! Lord, I stand in awe of Your heavenly reign. You are the ascended One, seated on the throne of heaven. I worship You, Jesus. As I meditate on this truth, I invite You to be the ascended Jesus in my own heart. May my life be ordered at the foot of Your throne. I surrender everything I have and am to You, trusting You to reign fully over my life. Awaken my heart with longing to see Your reign over all the earth, Jesus! May the reality of Your ascended glory be known throughout the globe. Amen.*

Encountering the *Ascended* Jesus:
A PRACTICAL APPLICATION

Remember—these four steps, as explained more fully on pages 23–24 in the introduction, are suggested to help you apply this quality of Christ to your own life.

1. **EXPLORE:** Take time to meditate on this quality of Christ. Use Scriptures in this chapter to get started.

2. **EXPERIENCE:** Turn your meditation into prayer that this quality might impact your life today. Pray the above prayer to begin.

3. **EXPRESS:** During your quiet time, take a moment to journal your thoughts, even if briefly.

4. **EXALT:** Pray, praise or even spontaneously sing your way through today's list of the names of Jesus. It only requires a few minutes.

GLORIFY HIS NAME

Through you we push back our enemies;
through your *name* we trample our foes.

PSALM 44:5 NIV, *emphasis added*

He Who Sits in the Heavens
Psalm 2:4 NKJV

Hidden Manna, The Revelation 2:17 NKJV

Hiding Place from the Wind, A
Isaiah 32:2 NKJV

Hiding Place in Tough Times, A
Nahum 1:7 MSG

High and Eternal Psalm 92:8 MSG

High and Exalted One Isaiah 57:15 NIV

High and Lofty One, The
Isaiah 57:15 NKJV

High and Towering God, The
Isaiah 57:15 MSG

**High Crag Where I Run for Dear
Life, The** Psalm 18:2 MSG

High God Psalm 9:2 MSG

High God of Israel, The
Psalm 68:34 MSG

High God of the Cosmos
Psalm 97:9 MSG

High King over All Gods
Psalm 95:3 MSG

High Rock Mountain Psalm 61:2 MSG

**Him Who Lives for an Eternity of
Eternities** Revelation 10:6 TPT

His Only Begotten Son John 3:16 NKJV

**His Wraparound Presence Always
Protects Me** Psalm 62:2 TPT

**Holds Everything Together by
What He Says** Hebrews 1:3 MSG

Holy Isaiah 6:3 KJV

Holy and Awe-Inspiring Psalm 111:9 NLT

Holy and Awesome Psalm 111:9 NIV

Holy and Dependable
Revelation 6:10 TPT

Holy and Righteous One, The
Acts 3:14 NIV

Holy and True Revelation 6:10 NKJV

Holy in Israel, The Ezekiel 39:7 MSG

Holy One, The Isaiah 57:15 NLT

Holy One and the Just, The
Acts 3:14 NKJV

Holy Sacrifice, A John 17:19 NLT

THE
HUMBLE
JESUS

Exploring the Wonders of Christ's Humility

> Humility is the only soil in which the graces root; the lack of humility is the sufficient explanation of every defect and failure.
>
> ANDREW MURRAY

CHARLES SPURGEON, preaching on the humility of Christ, provides an excellent place to begin our overview of the *Humble Jesus*. Spurgeon wrote:

> Infinite, and an infant. Eternal, and yet born of a woman. Almighty, and yet hanging on a woman's breast. Supporting a universe, and yet needing to be carried in a mother's arms. King of angels, and yet the reputed son of Joseph. Heir of all things, and yet the carpenter's despised son.[1]

Christ in His humanity, indeed, embodied the supremacy of humility. Even the prophets foretold the coming Messiah would be a humble king. Zechariah wrote:

> Shout and cheer, Daughter Zion! Raise the roof, Daughter Jerusalem! Your king is coming! a good king who makes all things right, a humble king riding a donkey, a mere colt of a donkey. I've

had it with war—no more chariots in Ephraim, no more war horses in Jerusalem, no more swords and spears, bows and arrows. He will offer peace to the nations, a peaceful rule worldwide, from the four winds to the seven seas.

ZECHARIAH 9:9–10 MSG

We see this prophecy fulfilled when Jesus enters Jerusalem in what is referred to as Christ's Triumphal Entry. Matthew would refer to Zechariah's prophecy when he later wrote:

This took place to fulfill the prophecy that said, "Tell the people of Jerusalem, 'Look, your King is coming to you. He is humble, riding on a donkey—riding on a donkey's colt.'"

MATTHEW 21:4–5 NLT

The Status of a Slave

Christ is the supreme example of humility through the very act of humbling Himself and leaving His heavenly position to come to earth as the supreme sacrifice for all of humankind. Paul spoke specifically of Christ's supreme humility when he wrote to the Philippian believers. He was admonishing them to view Christ as their ultimate example of living a life of humility. He wrote:

Think of yourselves the way Christ Jesus thought of himself. . . . He set aside the privileges of deity and took on the status of a slave, became *human*! Having become human, he stayed human. It was an incredibly humbling process.

PHILIPPIANS 2:5–8 MSG

Humility sometimes has a bad rap. Living a life of humility doesn't mean we are to become spiritual wimps. Later in our journey of exploring the wonders of Christ's nature, we will speak of His supreme authority. But even His authority was carried out in humility. *Humility* by definition is "the absence of vanity or excessive pride." Related to humility is meekness. *Meek* is defined as "being patient and mild; not inclined to anger or resentment; unassuming." Related qualities include "unobtrusiveness; unassuming; obscure; simple." Our Lord embodied all these qualities.

In Christ's Sermon on the Mount, we recall His prophetic promise for those who are meek: "Blessed are the meek, for they shall inherit the earth" (Matthew 5:5 NKJV). The New Living Translation employs the word *humble* in place of *meek*. It reads: "God blesses those who are humble, for they will inherit the whole earth." *The Message* offers: "You're blessed when you're content with just who you are—no more, no less. That's the moment you find yourselves proud owners of everything that can't be bought."

Few Christian authors over past generations have highlighted the quality of humility as much as Dutch missionary to Southern Africa Andrew Murray. In his book simply titled *Humility*, Murray summed up the humble Jesus in just ten words: "Christ is the humility of God embodied in human nature." The author then asks:

> What is the incarnation but His heavenly humility, His emptying Himself and becoming man? What is His life on earth but humility, His taking the form of a servant? And what is His atonement but humility? He humbled Himself and became obedient unto death. . . . He is the eternal love humbling itself, clothing itself in the garb of meekness and gentleness, to win and serve and save us.[2]

The Displacement of Self

The apostle Peter addressed the subject of humility when he wrote, "Finally, all of you, have unity of mind, sympathy, brotherly love, a tender heart, and a humble mind" (1 Peter 3:8 ESV). Here Peter reminds us that humility begins in the mind. It is where we cultivate our thoughts about our self-importance.

Peter's advice for the cultivation of humility is simple: "Clothe yourselves, all of you, with humility toward one another, for 'God opposes the proud but gives grace to the humble.' Humble yourselves, therefore, under the mighty hand of God so that at the proper time he may exalt you" (1 Peter 5:5–6 ESV). We likewise recall how Jesus chastised His disciples and others who had gathered around Him when He spoke of how the Pharisees love the place of highest honor at banquets and the most important seats in the synagogues. His response was a call for humility: "The greatest among you will be your servant. For those who exalt themselves will be humbled, and those who humble themselves will be exalted" (Matthew 23:11–12 NIV). The apostle James would later recall these words of Christ and remind believers:

> "God opposes the proud but gives grace to the humble." Submit yourselves therefore to God. Resist the devil, and he will flee from you. Draw near to God, and he will draw near to you. . . . Humble yourselves before the Lord, and he will exalt you.
>
> JAMES 4:6–8, 10 ESV

To those who would increasingly long to be like Jesus, living a blessed and holy life of humility, I would offer these concluding remarks from Andrew Murray:

> Humility . . . is the displacement of self by the enthronement of God. Where God is all, self is nothing. . . . Humility is not so much a grace or virtue along with others; it is the root of all, because it alone assumes the right attitude before God and allows him as God to do all.[3]

A PRAYER FOR TODAY

Today I come into Your presence, Jesus, to focus my heart and soul on Your humility. You gave up all of heaven and humbled Yourself, taking on human form to be my Savior. You walked among us in humility, never seeking fame or exaltation. You humbly died the lowliest of deaths upon the cross. I am undone by Your humility, Lord Jesus. I want to be more like You. I want to walk in Your humility. I bow my heart before You, Lord, and humbly surrender all things to You. Jesus, lead me in the ways of Your humility that I might bring You joy this day! Amen.

Encountering the Humble Jesus:
A PRACTICAL APPLICATION

Remember—these four steps, as explained more fully on pages 23–24 in the introduction, are suggested to help you apply this quality of Christ to your own life.

1. **EXPLORE:** Take time to meditate on this quality of Christ. Use Scriptures in this chapter to get started.

2. **EXPERIENCE:** Turn your meditation into prayer that this quality might impact your life today. Pray the above prayer to begin.

3. **EXPRESS:** During your quiet time, take a moment to journal your thoughts, even if briefly.

4. **EXALT:** Pray, praise or even spontaneously sing your way through today's list of the names of Jesus. It only requires a few minutes.

GLORIFY HIS NAME

Sing to the LORD, you saints of his; praise his holy *name*.

PSALM 30:4 NIV1984, *emphasis added*

Holy Watchman, A Daniel 4:13 MSG

Hope of Glory, The Colossians 1:27 NKJV

Hope of Israel, The Jeremiah 17:13 MSG

Hope of My Heart Psalm 42:11 NLT

Hope of Their Ancestors, The
Jeremiah 50:7 NIV

Hope of Their Fathers, The
Jeremiah 50:7 NKJV

Horn of Salvation, A Luke 1:69 NKJV

Huge Eagle Hovering in the Sky
Isaiah 31:5 MSG

Huge Granite Outcrop Giving
Shade in the Desert, A
Isaiah 32:2 MSG

I Am John 8:58 NLT

I-Am-Present Exodus 6:3 MSG

I-Am-Who-I-Am Exodus 3:14 MSG

Image of God, The
2 Corinthians 4:4 NKJV

Image of the Invisible God, The
Colossians 1:15 NKJV

Immanuel: God Is with Us
Matthew 1:23 NLT

Immortal 1 Timothy 1:17 MSG

Impregnable Castle, An Psalm 62:2 MSG

Incomparable, The Isaiah 46:5 MSG

Indescribable Gift 2 Corinthians 9:15 NIV

Indestructible, Invisible, and Full of
Glory 1 Timothy 1:17 TPT

Inspiration and Fountain of Hope
Romans 15:13 TPT

Invincible Commander of Heaven's
Hosts Psalm 24:10 TPT

Invisible 1 Timothy 1:17 MSG

Irreplaceable Isaiah 46:9 MSG

Israel's Guardian Psalm 121:4 MSG

Israel's Maker Isaiah 45:11 MSG

Israel's Personal God Zephaniah 2:9 MSG

THE
COMPASSIONATE
JESUS

Exploring the Wonders
of Christ's Compassion

Compassion is not pity. Compassion is love in action!

OSWALD J. SMITH

MOTHER TERESA WAS ONCE ASKED why she chose to go to Calcutta for ministry when it was considered to be the most impoverished city on earth. She responded, "I just followed Jesus, and that is where He led me."[1] The testimony of this humble saint is summed up in her personal manifesto: "Jesus is my God, Jesus is my Spouse, Jesus is my Life. Jesus is my only Love, Jesus is my All, Jesus is my Everything. Because of this I am never afraid. I am doing my work with Jesus. I am doing it for Jesus. I'm doing it to Jesus; therefore, the results are His, not mine."

Mother Teresa's inspiring testimony brings our Month in the Son journey to view the wonders of the *Compassionate Jesus*. She sums up this quality of Christ's incarnation succinctly: "Christ came to be Father's compassion to the world." As we looked at the humble Jesus in the previous chapter, it is understandable that the quality of compassion would logically follow. Humility births compassion. Again, as has been true of all of these qualities of Christ, Christ embodies the supremacy of compassion.

Love in Its Dynamic Phase

Compassion, by definition, is "to feel or express sorrow for the sufferings or troubles of another, usually accompanied by an urge to help." It is also defined as, "Deep sympathy or pity for the suffering of others." Related to compassion are: "kindness, thoughtfulness, forbearance, understanding, and tenderness." *Compassion* is derived from the two Latin words *com* and *pati—com* meaning "with" or "together," and *pati* meaning "to suffer" or "to hurt." Combined, these expressions describe a person who *"suffers with"* someone in need or *"hurts together"* with those undergoing suffering.

Jesus personified a lifestyle of compassion. Matthew describes Christ moving through the countryside, going from village to village "healing every sickness and every disease among the people" (Matthew 9:35 NKJV). Matthew continues: "But when He saw the multitudes, He was moved with compassion for them, because they were weary and scattered, like sheep having no shepherd" (Matthew 9:36 NKJV). The expression "moved with compassion" indicates a compassion that necessitates action.

In describing yet another occasion of Christ interacting with a crowd, Matthew records:

> Then Jesus called His disciples to Him and said, I have pity and sympathy and am deeply moved for the crowd, because they have been with Me now three days and they have nothing [at all left] to eat; and I am not willing to send them away hungry, lest they faint or become exhausted on the way.
>
> MATTHEW 15:32 AMPC

Again, we see Christ being "deeply moved" and expressing both pity and sympathy for the multitudes.

Compassion, of course, is more than mere pity, though a sense of pity often is involved. But it is not a pity that looks on from a distance. Compassion is pity that takes one to the point of another's need. It is love in its dynamic phase, love released through action. It is a life of involvement in the struggles and challenges of others. A memorable line from the pen of composer Oscar Hammerstein II highlights this reality: "Love in your heart wasn't put there to stay—love isn't love 'til you give it away."[2]

Compassion in Action

Jesus was not an intercessor only when He prayed. He lived a life of intercession. Jesus is the embodiment of compassion. When He prayed, it was compassion praying. When He healed, it was compassion healing. When He cast out demons, it was compassionate deliverance. When the physician Luke wrote in Acts that Jesus went about doing good, healing all those who were oppressed (Acts 10:38), it was a picture of compassionate action. The same could be said of Christ's prayers. As I stated in my book *Love on Its Knees* (Chosen Books, 1989), to see Christ at prayer is to see love on its knees. To see Christ doing ministry is to see compassion in action! Christ gave us the supreme expression of compassion in action when He went to the cross to remove the suffering brought on humankind through sin.

We serve the same Jesus who walked the rolling hillsides of Galilee two thousand years ago. He was and is the compassionate One. Jeremiah spoke of the unfailing compassion of our Lord hundreds of years before Christ's birth, and this compassion is still as great today as it was when Jeremiah penned these words: "This I recall to my mind, therefore have I hope. It is of the Lord's mercies that we are not consumed, because his compassions fail not. They are new every morning: great is thy faithfulness" (Lamentations 3:21–23 KJV).

The Message offers this paraphrase of Jeremiah's remorseful reflections in Lamentations 3:21–23:

> I'll never forget the trouble, the utter lostness. . . . I remember it all—the feeling of hitting the bottom. But there's one other thing I remember, and remembering, I keep a grip on hope: God's loyal love couldn't have run out, his merciful love couldn't have dried up. They're created new every morning. How great your faithfulness!

Christ's compassion, of course, was a costly compassion. The cost was the cross! Compassion implies giving oneself away, and there is always a cost to giving. There must be no hoarders of compassion in the Kingdom. To share Christ's compassion is to become Christ's extended hands to a hurting and suffering world. Mystic Teresa of Avila, a Carmelite nun in the sixteenth century, leaves us these parting words: "Christ has no body now on earth but yours, no hands, no feet but yours. Yours are the eyes with which Christ looks out His compassion to the world. Yours are the feet with which He is to go about doing good. Yours are the hands with which He is to bless us now."[3]

A PRAYER FOR TODAY

As I bow before You today, Lord Jesus, I humbly receive *Your compassion for me. I bring all of my need, my trauma, my wounds and my chronic suffering into Your presence. Oh, how I need Your loving compassion. I invite Your healing gaze upon all my cares. I welcome You into my grieving and the lifelong journey of my healing and seeking to become like You. I receive Your love and affection in the midst of it all. I trust, Lord Jesus, that as I receive Your compassion, I will be a vessel to carry it to others, always ready to pour out Your compassion upon all those around me. Amen.*

Encountering the *Compassionate* Jesus:
A PRACTICAL APPLICATION

Remember—these four steps, as explained more fully on pages 23–24 in the introduction, are suggested to help you apply this quality of Christ to your own life.

1. **EXPLORE:** Take time to meditate on this quality of Christ. Use Scriptures in this chapter to get started.

2. **EXPERIENCE:** Turn your meditation into prayer that this quality might impact your life today. Pray the above prayer to begin.

3. **EXPRESS:** During your quiet time, take a moment to journal your thoughts, even if briefly.

4. **EXALT:** Pray, praise or even spontaneously sing your way through today's list of the names of Jesus. It only requires a few minutes.

GLORIFY HIS NAME

In God we make our boast all day long, and
we will praise your *name* forever.

Psalm 44:8 NIV, *emphasis added*

Israel's Strong God Psalm 68:35 MSG

Jacob-Wrestling God Psalm 46:11 MSG

Jehovah-Elohay: Lord My God
Zechariah 14:5 NKJV

**Jehovah-Eloheka: The Lord Your
God** Exodus 20:2 NKJV

**Jehovah-Elohim: The Eternal
Creator** Genesis 2:4-25 NLT

**Jehovah-Elyon: The Lord Most
High** Psalm 7:17 NLT

**Jehovah-Hosenu: The Lord Our
Maker** Psalm 95:6 NLT

**Jehovah-Jireh: The Lord Will
Provide** Genesis 22:14 NLT

**Jehovah-Mekaddishkem: The
Lord Who Makes You Holy**
Leviticus 20:8 NLT

Jehovah-Nissi: The Lord My Banner
Exodus 17:15 NKJV

**Jehovah-Rohi: The Lord My
Shepherd** Psalm 23:1 NKJV

**Jehovah-Ropheka: The Lord Who
Heals You** Exodus 15:26 NLT

**Jehovah-Sabaoth: The Lord of
Heaven's Armies** 1 Samuel 1:3 NLT

**Jehovah-Shalom: The Lord Is
Peace** Judges 6:24 NLT

**Jehovah-Shammah: The Lord Is
There** Ezekiel 48:35 NLT

**Jehovah-Tsidkenu: The Lord Is Our
Righteousness** Jeremiah 23:6 NLT

Jesse's Root Isaiah 11:10 MSG

Jesus Christ the Righteous
1 John 2:1 NKJV

Jesus—God Saves Matthew 1:21 MSG

Judge and Lawgiver Isaiah 33:22 NKJV

Judge of the Earth Psalm 94:2 MSG

Judge of the Living and Dead
Acts 10:42 MSG

Judge over All Things
Hebrews 12:23 NLT

Just One, The Acts 7:52 NKJV

Kernel of Wheat, A John 12:23-24 NLT

Kind and Tenderhearted
Psalm 103:8 TPT

**Kind Guardian Who Lovingly
Watches over Your Souls**
1 Peter 2:25 TPT

Kind One, The Psalm 141:5 MSG

THE
MERCIFUL
JESUS

Exploring the Wonders of Christ's Mercies

There is more mercy in Christ than sin in us.

RICHARD SIBBES

ONE DROP OF THE LORD'S MERCY is better than an ocean of the world's comfort."[1] These words of Lysa TerKeurst bring us to today's view of our supreme Savior as the *Merciful Jesus*! The name *Jesus* is quite simply synonymous with the word *mercy*. *Mercy* is defined as "kindness shown in excess of what might be expected; forbearance." Merciful is an especially important descriptive word when looking at the nature and character of Christ. *Merciful* means "to be full of mercy; having, feeling or showing mercy." It is basically "the giving of a second chance." The whole of Christ's incarnation is a picture of His mercy. In a true sense, it was God's merciful forgiveness that was manifested in Christ's incarnation. Our Month in the Son, therefore, would be incomplete without encountering afresh our Lord as the *Merciful Jesus*.

Full of Second Chances

Long a favorite Scripture passage of mine that some might refer to as a "life passage" is the psalmist's prayer in Psalm 67. Note especially the first two verses from the King James Version, the translation that was the focus of my Bible memorization in my younger years. The psalmist prayed: "God be merciful unto us, and bless us; and cause his face to shine upon us; Selah. That thy way may be known upon earth, thy saving health among all nations" (Psalm 67:1–2 KJV).

Notice how the psalmist begins by pleading for God to be merciful. *Mercy* is, as I suggested earlier, "the giving of a second chance." *Full*, as was also mentioned, means "having in it all there is space for." Our Lord is wonderfully merciful! He is full of second chances. That is truly Good News for humans prone to sin like you and me. I am sure you can testify, as can I, that God has given me many second chances.

The author of Hebrews especially calls our attention to this great quality of the life of Christ. He writes:

> We also know that the Son did not come to help angels; he came to help the descendants of Abraham. Therefore, it was necessary for him to be made in every respect like us, his brothers and sisters, so that he could be our merciful and faithful High Priest before God. Then he could offer a sacrifice that would take away the sins of the people.
>
> HEBREWS 2:16–17 NLT

The Marvelous Miracle of Mercy

The mercy of our Lord is a wonderful theme throughout the Scriptures. The psalmist declared: "The name of the Lord is blessed and lifted high! For his marvelous miracle of mercy protected me when I was overwhelmed by my enemies" (Psalm 31:21 TPT). Elsewhere he prayed, "Forgive my failures as a young man, and overlook the sins of my immaturity. Give me grace, Lord! Always look at me through your eyes of love—your forgiving eyes of mercy and compassion.... How good you are to me!" (Psalm 25:6–7 TPT).

In Paul's letter to Titus, the apostle wanted his partner in ministry to understand that our salvation was not based on our righteous activities but on the grace and mercy of Christ. He wrote: "But when the kindness and love of God our Savior appeared, he saved us, not because of righteous things we had done, but because of his mercy" (Titus 3:4–5 NIV). May we ever be cautious to recognize it isn't our efforts that bring us victoriously through our many tests and trials. It is the supreme mercy of Christ that sustains us. As T. D. Jakes reminds believers: "God's grace and mercy have brought you through. Quit acting as if you made it on your own."[2]

In writing his first letter to Timothy, Paul emphasized how thankful he was for Christ's mercy in light of the fact he openly blasphemed the Lord and persecuted believers before his conversion. He confessed:

> I thank Christ Jesus our Lord, who has given me strength, that he considered me trustworthy, appointing me to his service. Even though I was once a blasphemer and a persecutor and a violent man, I was shown mercy because I acted in ignorance and unbelief. The grace of our Lord was poured out on me abundantly, along with the faith and love that are in Christ Jesus.
>
> 1 TIMOTHY 1:12–14 NIV

Paul had experienced, firsthand, the marvelous miracle of the Lord's mercy.

Paul provides a fitting conclusion to our overview of the *Merciful Jesus* as he reflects with the Ephesian believers on God's immense mercy and incredible love:

> It wasn't so long ago that you were mired in that old stagnant life of sin. You let the world, which doesn't know the first thing about living, tell you how to live. You filled your lungs with polluted unbelief, and then exhaled disobedience. . . . It's a wonder God didn't lose his temper and do away with the whole lot of us. Instead, immense in mercy and with an incredible love, he embraced us. He took our sin-dead lives and made us alive in Christ.
>
> EPHESIANS 2:1–2, 3, 5 MSG

Have you thanked the Lord today for His mercy? What a great way to start a day! Wise is the challenge of Charles Spurgeon: "The first fresh hour of every morning should be dedicated to the Lord, whose mercy gladdens it with golden light."[3]

A PRAYER FOR TODAY

Jesus — most merciful lord — I come before You today in desperate need of Your great and abundant mercy. As I fix my attention upon You, Lord, I become even more aware of my needs. I bring my sin, my pain, my suffering, my wounds, my failures and all my shame into the light of Your presence, for Your very presence, O Lord, is the abundance of mercy. I cry out to You in my lack. I need Your mercy, Jesus. I so need Your second chances. As I receive Your loving mercy, I invite You to transform my heart as I rest these moments in Your presence. And may I become a conduit of Your mercy to others, O Lord, who are in desperate need at this hour. Thank You, Jesus, most merciful Lord. Amen.

Encountering the *Merciful* Jesus:
A PRACTICAL APPLICATION

Remember—these four steps, as explained more fully on pages 23-24 in the introduction, are suggested to help you apply this quality of Christ to your own life.

1. **EXPLORE:** Take time to meditate on this quality of Christ. Use Scriptures in this chapter to get started.

2. **EXPERIENCE:** Turn your meditation into prayer that this quality might impact your life today. Pray the above prayer to begin.

3. **EXPRESS:** During your quiet time, take a moment to journal your thoughts, even if briefly.

4. **EXALT:** Pray, praise or even spontaneously sing your way through today's list of the names of Jesus. It only requires a few minutes.

GLORIFY HIS NAME

I will praise you forever for what you have done;
in your *name* I will hope, for your *name* is good. I
will praise you in the presence of your saints.

PSALM 52:9 NIV1984, *emphasis added*

King, The Zechariah 14:16 NKJV

King from the East Isaiah 41:2 NLT

King-Glory Psalm 24:7 MSG

King-God over All Other Gods
Psalm 95:3 TPT

King in All His Splendor, The
Isaiah 33:17 NLT

King in His Beauty, The Isaiah 33:17 NKJV

King in Zion, A Psalm 2:6 MSG

King of All Kings Revelation 17:14 NLT

King of All Time, The 1 Timothy 1:17 MSG

King of Glory, The Psalm 24:10 NLT

King of Heaven, The Daniel 4:34 MSG

King of Israel, The John 1:49 NKJV

King of Jacob, The Isaiah 41:21 NKJV

King of Kings Revelation 19:16 MSG

King of Peace Hebrews 7:2 NKJV

King of Righteousness Hebrews 7:2 NKJV

King of the Nations Revelation 15:3 NLT

King of the Saints Revelation 15:3 NKJV

King over All the Earth
Zechariah 14:9 NLT

King-Priest Forever Hebrews 5:6 TPT

King's Son, The Psalm 72:1 NKJV

King Who Rules with Wisdom, A
Jeremiah 23:5 NLT

**King Who Shall Reign and Prosper,
A** Jeremiah 23:5 NKJV

King Who Will Reign Wisely, A
Jeremiah 23:5 NIV

**King Who Will Rule in the Right
Way, A** Isaiah 32:1 MSG

**Lamb in the Midst of the Throne,
The** Revelation 7:17 NKJV

Lamb Is Its Light, The
Revelation 21:23 NKJV

Lamb of God, The John 1:29 NLT

THE
ABIDING
JESUS

Exploring the Wonders of Christ's Presence

As you walk through the valley of the unknown, you will find the footprints of Jesus both in front of you and beside you.

CHARLES STANLEY

O. HALLESBY, respected Norwegian theologian in the first half of the twentieth century, wrote: "Jesus wants to see to it that your religion becomes something more than mere longing and sighing. He Himself will come in and abide with you."[1]

This brings us during our Month in the Son to our consideration of Christ's supreme presence as the *Abiding Jesus*. The apostle John records these words of Christ that are both cautionary and encouraging:

> "I am the sprouting vine and you're my branches. As you live in union with me as your source, fruitfulness will stream from within you—but when you live separated from me you are powerless.... But if you live in life-union with me and if my words live powerfully within you—then you can ask whatever you desire and it will be done. When your lives bear abundant fruit, you demonstrate that you are my mature disciples who glorify my Father!"
>
> JOHN 15:5, 7–8 TPT

The Message offers this paraphrase of these same words of Christ from John 15:

> I've loved you the way my Father has loved me. Make yourselves at home in my love. If you keep my commands, you'll remain intimately at home in my love. That's what I've done—kept my Father's commands and made myself at home in his love.
>
> JOHN 15:9–10 MSG

Here again we are introduced to the *Abiding Jesus*. Earlier He had told His disciples, "Loving me empowers you to obey my word. And my Father will love you so deeply that we will come to you and make you our dwelling place" (John 14:23 TPT).

The Pleasures of God's Presence

The sense of Christ abiding in us, and our abiding in His Word, is much more than a mere spiritual exercise of taking a few moments here and there to read our Bibles or to voice a casual prayer now and then. To abide suggests taking up residence in a place with the intention to permanently dwell there. Christ has promised to permanently dwell in our hearts as we permanently dwell in His Word. Note again these words from John 15 from *The Message*: "Make yourselves at home in my love." This is followed by the powerful promise of Christ: "If you keep my commands, you'll remain intimately at home in my love" (verses 9–10). This is the essence of abiding. Caryll Houselander described this lifestyle thus: "Christ asks for a home in your soul where he can be at rest with you, where he can talk easily to you, where you and he, alone together, can laugh and be silent and be delighted with one another."[2]

We recall how Christ told His disciples: "I call you my most intimate friends, for I reveal to you everything that I've heard from my Father" (John 15:15 TPT). Commenting on this passage, evangelist Dwight L. Moody testified: "A rule I have had for years is to treat the Lord Jesus Christ as a personal friend. He is not a creed, a mere doctrine, but it is He Himself we have."[3] A. W. Tozer spoke of the pleasures of abiding in our Lord when he wrote: "Nothing in or of this world measures up to the simple pleasure of experiencing the presence of God."[4] There are, indeed, no pleasures in life that can compare to the pleasures of God's presence!

The Unforced Rhythms of Grace

These are truly trying times, and it is easy for believers, even those who have served Christ for many years, to grow weary. Only in walking daily with the *Abiding Jesus* will we find the spiritual energy to continue. In our weariness, we hear the comforting words of Christ recorded in Matthew's gospel:

> "Are you tired? Worn out? Burned out on religion? Come to me. Get away with me and you'll recover your life. I'll show you how to take a real rest. Walk with me and work with me—watch how I do it. Learn the unforced rhythms of grace. I won't lay anything heavy or ill-fitting on you. Keep company with me and you'll learn to live freely and lightly."
>
> MATTHEW 11:28–30 MSG

To experience Christ's "unforced rhythms of grace," we must cultivate a daily intimacy with Him. To truly know the *Abiding Christ*, He must abide in us and we must abide in Him. We recall how Moses admonished God's people: "Serve only the Lord your God and fear him alone. Obey his commands, listen to his voice, and cling to him" (Deuteronomy 13:4 NLT). To *cling* means "to hold fast by or as by embracing, entwining, or sticking." George Müller, whom I have mentioned elsewhere in this book, lived a life of extraordinary faith in caring for thousands of orphans in nineteenth-century England. He provides a worthy conclusion to our overview of the *Abiding Jesus*:

> He, my Friend, my Lord, my Savior, my Bridegroom, is the mighty God. *I* am perfect weakness, *I* cannot stand against my enemies. *I* am helpless. Oh, how weak, how extremely weak am *I* in myself! But if I cling to the mighty God, He is able and willing to help me. He proved the depth of His love to me by laying down His life for me, a miserable guilty sinner. He, our best Friend, our bosom Friend, is at the same time the mighty God. Oh! Let us cling to the mighty God.[5]

A PRAYER FOR TODAY

Jesus, daily I long for a deeper intimacy with You. As I meditate on the word abide *today, my heart comes alive to a consciousness of Your nearness. I pray, Jesus, that I would grow continually in my awareness of Your presence in and around me. May I be awakened to Your voice, Your heart, Your wonder alive in me. May I be sensitive and attentive to Your abiding in my own soul. I want to abide in Your Word, more aware every moment of Your love. May I become someone who lives ever more fully in the reality of Your abiding truth. Amen.*

Encountering the *Abiding* Jesus:
A PRACTICAL APPLICATION

Remember—these four steps, as explained more fully on pages 23–24 in the introduction, are suggested to help you apply this quality of Christ to your own life.

1. **EXPLORE:** Take time to meditate on this quality of Christ. Use Scriptures in this chapter to get started.

2. **EXPERIENCE:** Turn your meditation into prayer that this quality might impact your life today. Pray the above prayer to begin.

3. **EXPRESS:** During your quiet time, take a moment to journal your thoughts, even if briefly.

4. **EXALT:** Pray, praise or even spontaneously sing your way through today's list of the names of Jesus. It only requires a few minutes.

GLORIFY HIS NAME

Sing the glory of his *name*; make his praise glorious!

PSALM 66:2 NIV1984, *emphasis added*

Lamb on the Throne Revelation 7:17 MSG

Lamb Taken to Be Slaughtered, A
Isaiah 53:7 MSG

Lamb Who Was Slain, The
Revelation 5:12 NKJV

Lamb without Blemish, A
1 Peter 1:19 NKJV

Last Revelation 1:17 MSG

Last to Leave, The Isaiah 41:4 MSG

Last Word, The John 12:48 MSG

Lawgiver Isaiah 33:22 NLT

Leader among the Nations, A
Isaiah 55:4 NLT

Leader Who Will Shepherd-Rule
Israel, The Micah 5:4 MSG

Leader You Have Been Looking
For, The Malachi 3:1 MSG

Life-Giving God Luke 1:47 TPT

Life-Giving Spirit, A
1 Corinthians 15:45 NKJV

Life-Giving Strength Psalm 62:7 TPT

Life, Life, and More Life
Isaiah 53:10 MSG

Life-Light, The John 1:4 MSG

Lifetime Pass to Your Safe-House,
A Psalm 61:3 MSG

Light by Which We See Psalm 36:9 NLT

Light for All Humanity John 1:4 TPT

Light for the Nations, A Isaiah 49:6 MSG

Light of Israel, The Isaiah 10:17 NLT

Light of Men, The John 1:4 NKJV

Light of Revelation Psalm 36:9 TPT

Light of the City Revelation 21:23 NLT

Light of the Morning, The
2 Samuel 23:4 NKJV

Light of the World, The John 8:12 NLT

Light of Truth John 1:9 TPT

Light to Everyone John 1:4 NLT

THE
SPOTLESS
JESUS

Exploring the Wonders of Christ's Holiness

> There is only one Being who can live the Sermon on the Mount and that is the Son of God!
>
> OSWALD CHAMBERS

NOTHING COUNTS WITH GOD, except His beloved Son, Jesus Christ, who is completely pure and holy before Him. Where He is, there God looks and has His pleasure."[1] With these words from the pen of Martin Luther, we come to explore the wonders of the *Spotless Jesus*. Of all the billions of human beings ever to walk the earth, only one was perfect—absolutely *spotless* and unconditionally *holy* by any definition mortal man might give to the words *spotless* and *holy*.

Spotless seems to define itself. It simply means "having no spots." A fuller definition reads: "perfectly clean; having no faults or defects, as in character or behavior." There are numerous synonyms we might add to this, including "irreproachable; stainless; immaculate, without blemish, untarnished, unsullied, uncontaminated; pure and reliable."

The Personification of Perfection

This is Jesus, supreme in His perfection! He is, indeed, the *Spotless Jesus*. Of this quality of Christ, Billy Graham wrote: "As I read the Bible, I seem to find holiness to be [Christ's] supreme attribute."[2] A broader biblical word to describe the lifestyle of Jesus is, of course, *holy*. To speak of Christ as holy, or the perfect picture of holiness, we are speaking of One who is "spiritually perfect or pure; untainted by evil or sin; morally complete in every way." Our word *holy* comes from the Middle English word *hool*, meaning "healthy, unhurt, entire." Those words come from the Old English *hal*, meaning "sound or whole." Probing just a bit deeper, the word *whole* means "constituting the total sum or undiminished entirety; the entirety of a person's nature; free of defect or impairment."

The apostle Peter simply described our spotless Savior thus: "He never sinned, nor ever deceived anyone. He did not retaliate when he was insulted, nor threaten revenge when he suffered. He left his case in the hands of God who always judges fairly" (1 Peter 2:22–23 NLT). *The Message* provides this unique paraphrase of verses 21–23:

> This is the kind of life you've been invited into, the kind of life Christ lived. He suffered everything that came his way so you would know that it could be done, and also know how to do it, step-by-step. He never did one thing wrong, not once said anything amiss. They called him every name in the book and he said nothing back. He suffered in silence, content to let God set things right.

Earlier in our study in looking at both the *Human Jesus* and the *Divine Jesus*, we established that Christ's incarnation was God Himself becoming man. Thus, Christ brought all the perfections of God the Father to planet earth. The perfections of God were clearly in Christ as

He lived out His humanity. Christ was, quite simply, the personification of perfection.

The apostle Peter in his two letters to Jewish converts scattered throughout the then-evangelized provinces said much about the *Spotless Jesus* and our need as followers of Christ to embrace such a life of holiness. Early in his first letter, Peter wrote:

> So prepare your minds for action and exercise self-control. Put all your hope in the gracious salvation that will come to you when Jesus Christ is revealed to the world. . . . But now you must be holy in everything you do, just as God who chose you is holy. For the Scriptures say, "You must be holy because I am holy."
>
> 1 Peter 1:13, 15–16 NLT

Later in the same letter, Peter reminded his readers of the supreme sacrifice Christ made on their behalf. Note this paraphrase from *The Message*:

> Your life is a journey you must travel with a deep consciousness of God. It cost God plenty to get you out of that dead-end, empty-headed life you grew up in. He paid with Christ's sacred blood, you know. He died like an unblemished, sacrificial lamb.
>
> 1 Peter 1:18–19 MSG

Destined for Holiness

Some Bible teachers, when speaking of living a life of holiness, refer to it as a life of sanctification, or being fully set apart and pure in one's Christian walk. Oswald Chambers, author of the timeless classic *My Utmost for His Highest*, wrote: "Sanctification does not mean anything less than the holiness of Jesus being made mine manifestly. . . . It means being made one with Jesus. Sanctification is not something Jesus Christ puts into me: It is Himself in me."[3]

The apostle Paul made it clear that living such a sanctified life, with the *Spotless Jesus* always by our side, was not only the believer's calling, but it was the believer's destiny. Quite simply, we are destined for holiness. Paul wrote:

> Blessed be the God and Father of our Lord Jesus Christ, who has blessed us with every spiritual blessing in the heavenly places in Christ, just as He chose us in Him before the foundation of the world, that we would be holy and blameless before Him.
>
> EPHESIANS 1:3–4 NASB

Years ago, I wrestled with the issue of what personal holiness is. I became convinced it is not seeking to maintain a lengthy, legalistic list of things we can or cannot do in order to be holy. To me, holiness was to get so close to Jesus that any such list no longer mattered. I just wanted to be with Jesus. I just wanted to be like Jesus. I came to this conclusion: The more one has of Jesus, the more one has of His holiness. We just need more of Jesus!

A PRAYER FOR TODAY

O spotless Jesus — holy One — I come into Your presence today with my heart fixed upon Your holiness. You are blameless, perfect in every way, completely without sin. You are righteous and upright. Only as the spotless One could You rescue all Your people from the powers of death and sin. I honor You, Jesus. I thank You. I pray that

You would make me like You, Jesus, holy and pure. As You wash me clean by Your perfect blood, may I know Your ways and walk in them. May I be more fully conformed to Your image. May my life be spotless before You because of Your sacrifice on the cross for me. Thank You, holy Jesus. Amen.

Encountering the *Spotless* Jesus:
A PRACTICAL APPLICATION

Remember—these four steps, as explained more fully on pages 23–24 in the introduction, are suggested to help you apply this quality of Christ to your own life.

1. **EXPLORE:** Take time to meditate on this quality of Christ. Use Scriptures in this chapter to get started.

2. **EXPERIENCE:** Turn your meditation into prayer that this quality might impact your life today. Pray the above prayer to begin.

3. **EXPRESS:** During your quiet time, take a moment to journal your thoughts, even if briefly.

4. **EXALT:** Pray, praise or even spontaneously sing your way through today's list of the names of Jesus. It only requires a few minutes.

GLORIFY HIS NAME

I will sacrifice a freewill offering to you; I will
praise your *name*, O LORD, for it is good.

PSALM 54:6 NIV1984, *emphasis added*

Light to Guide the Nations, A
Luke 2:32 NLT

Light to Live By, The John 1:4 MSG

Light to the Gentiles, A
Isaiah 42:6 NKJV

Lily of the Valleys, The
Song of Solomon 2:1 NKJV

Lion of the Tribe of Judah, The
Revelation 5:5 NKJV

Living Bread, The John 6:51 NLT

Living Cornerstone, The 1 Peter 2:4 NLT

Living God, The Jeremiah 10:10 MSG

Living Stone, The 1 Peter 2:4 MSG

**Longsuffering and Abundant in
Mercy and Truth** Psalm 86:15 NKJV

Lord and Savior, Jesus Christ
2 Peter 3:18 NKJV

Lord from Heaven, The
1 Corinthians 15:47 NKJV

Lord God of Hosts Psalm 59:5 NKJV

Lord God Omnipotent, The
Revelation 19:6 NKJV

Lord God, the Almighty, The
Revelation 4:8 NLT

Lord Invincible in Battle, The
Psalm 24:8 NLT

Lord Is Good, The Psalm 100:5 NIV

**Lord Is Gracious and
Compassionate, The** Psalm 111:4 NIV

**Lord Jehovah from the Realm of
Heaven** 1 Corinthians 15:47 TPT

Lord Mighty in Battle, The
Psalm 24:8 NIV

Lord Most High, The Psalm 47:2 NLT

Lord of All Acts 10:36 NLT

Lord of All the Earth, The
Zechariah 6:5 NLT

**Lord of Both the Dead and the
Living** Romans 14:9 NKJV

Lord of Hosts, The Psalm 24:10 NKJV

Lord of Lords Revelation 17:14 NKJV

Lord of Peace, The
2 Thessalonians 3:16 NIV

Lord of Victory Psalm 24:10 TPT

Day 16

THE
MISSIONAL
JESUS

Exploring the Wonders of Christ's Mission

God had an only Son, and He was a missionary, and physician.

DAVID LIVINGSTON

JESUS CHRIST BECAME INCARNATE for one purpose, to make a way back to God that man might stand before Him as He was created to do, the friend and lover of God Himself!"[1] So describes Oswald Chambers in introducing us to the *Missional Jesus*. Henry Martyn, an Anglican missionary to India in the early 1800s, said: "The spirit of Christ is the spirit of missions. The nearer we get to Him, the more intensely missionary we become."[2]

David Livingston was correct: God's only Son was, indeed, a missionary, as well as a physician. Christ was sent to earth by His Father on a mission. *Mission*, by definition, means "a sending out or being sent out with authority to perform a specific task or service." It can also mean "a goal or objective to which a person or group is especially dedicated." The English word for *mission* comes from the Latin word *missio*—meaning "a task assigned; a sending away for a special duty or function for which a person is thought or considered to be destined;

a calling (i.e., one's mission in life)." It is the act of sending; from the Latin *mittere*, "to send."

No One Left Behind

The word *missional* is not generally found in dictionaries, but it has been coined by Christian missiologists to describe a person or a ministry that is especially focused on missions or deeply committed to a specific calling or a task related to a global spreading of the Gospel. It refers to ministries, organizations or causes that are mission-focused or mission-minded. Christ was and is clearly missional. Peter, in preaching his powerful message on the Day of Pentecost, told crowds: "Jesus, the Victorious, was a Man on a divine mission whose authority was clearly proven. For you know how God performed many powerful miracles, signs, and wonders through him" (Acts 2:22 TPT).

Christ made His mission clear when He told a large crowd following Him:

> "I came down from heaven not to follow my own whim but to accomplish the will of the One who sent me. This, in a nutshell, is that will: that everything handed over to me by the Father be completed. . . . This is what my Father wants: that anyone who sees the Son and trusts who he is and what he does and then aligns with him will enter *real* life, *eternal* life. My part is to put them on their feet alive and whole at the completion of time."
>
> JOHN 6:38–40 MSG

On one occasion, as recorded in Mark's gospel, Jesus had been doing many miracles in the city of Capernaum. But Christ knew it was time to move on. His mission was calling Him. When His disciples told Him that many more in the village desiring healing wanted Him to stay and continue His ministry, Jesus responded, "We have to go on to the surrounding villages so that I can give my message to the people there, for that is my mission" (Mark 1:38 TPT). Christ's mission was a harvest mission. No village was to be missed. No one was to be left behind! All must hear the Good News.

The Mantle of a Mission

Christ is especially specific about His missional mandate in His longest recorded prayer (John 17). Note His reference to His mission in these passages from *The Message* as relates to His disciples:

> "In the same way that you gave me a mission in the world, I give them a mission in the world. I'm consecrating myself for their sakes so they'll be truth-consecrated in their mission. . . . Righteous Father, the world has never known you, but I have known you, and these disciples know that you sent me on this mission."
>
> JOHN 17:18–19, 25 MSG

Christ's mission is now our mandate. He has passed the mantle of His mission to His obedient children who are willing to fulfill it. We recall how Christ appeared to His disciples after His resurrection. They were clustered together, fearful of reprisals from Jewish authorities. As they hid behind closed doors, Christ suddenly appeared. First, He encouraged them: "Peace to you!" Then He commissioned them: "Just as the Father has sent me, I'm now sending you" (John 20:21 TPT). If you are a believer, you are both called and commissioned. The mantle of Christ's mission has been passed to you.

William Booth, founder of the Salvation Army, was troubled by those who said they were not called to Christian service. One can almost imagine Booth's eyes flashing fire as he responded:

> "Not called!" did you say? Put your ear down to the Bible, and hear Him bid you go and pull sinners out of the fire of sin. Put your ear down to the burdened, agonized heart of humanity, and listen to its pitiful wail for help. . . . Then look Christ in the face . . . and tell Him whether you will join heart and soul and body and circumstances in the march to publish His mercy to the world.[3]

If we have seen the Light, we need to shine the Light! The apostle Paul wrote: "Once your life was full of sin's darkness, but now you have the very light of our Lord shining through you because of your union with him. Your mission is to live as children flooded with his revelation-light!" (Ephesians 5:8 TPT). John Keith Falconer, nineteenth-century Scottish missionary and Arabic scholar, wisely testified, "I have but one candle of life to burn, and I would rather burn it out in a land filled with darkness than in a land flooded with light."[4]

Where will your candle burn today? Have you thought about today's mission for your life? The *Missional Jesus* is ready to walk with you into your mission for today!

A PRAYER FOR TODAY

Gracious Savior, Lord of all, thank You for fulfilling Your divine mission to reconcile the world unto Your Father. Thank You for doing only the Father's will—and taking every fateful step that led You to the cross. Jesus, I know You have called me to carry on this mission to advance Your Kingdom both near and far. I pray today that You would bring clarity to my calling and faith to my focus: empower me to boldly fulfill Your will for my life. Make me sensitive to Your voice. I submit my life to You, committing all my days to advance Your mission in our hurting world. Amen.

Encountering the *Missional* Jesus:
A PRACTICAL APPLICATION

Remember—these four steps, as explained more fully on pages 23–24 in the introduction, are suggested to help you apply this quality of Christ to your own life.

1. **EXPLORE:** Take time to meditate on this quality of Christ. Use Scriptures in this chapter to get started.

2. **EXPERIENCE:** Turn your meditation into prayer that this quality might impact your life today. Pray the above prayer to begin.

3. **EXPRESS:** During your quiet time, take a moment to journal your thoughts, even if briefly.

4. **EXALT:** Pray, praise or even spontaneously sing your way through today's list of the names of Jesus. It only requires a few minutes.

GLORIFY HIS NAME

May his *name* endure forever; may it continue
as long as the sun. All nations will be blessed
through him, and they will call him blessed.

PSALM 72:17 NIV1984, *emphasis added*

Lord Our Maker, The Psalm 95:6 NKJV

Lord Our Righteousness, The
Jeremiah 23:6 NKJV

Lord over All Romans 10:12 NKJV

Lord Strong and Mighty, The
Psalm 24:8 NKJV

Lord Who Created the Heavens,
The Isaiah 45:18 NKJV

Lord Who Made You and Helps
You, The Isaiah 44:2 NLT

Lord Yahweh, The Romans 10:13 TPT

Lord Your Redeemer, The
Isaiah 43:14 NKJV

Lover of Justice Psalm 99:4 MSG

Loving Friend Who Is Joined to
Your Heart Proverbs 18:24 TPT

Loving Shepherd of Israel
Psalm 80:1 TPT

Loyal Always and Ever Psalm 100:5 MSG

Loyal Witness Revelation 1:5 MSG

Luxuriant Fruit Tree, A Hosea 14:8 MSG

Magnificent God Psalm 43:4 MSG

Magnificent King-Priest
Hebrews 4:14 TPT

Main Character in This Drama, The
Matthew 3:11 MSG

Majestic Lord, The Isaiah 33:21 NKJV

Maker Isaiah 17:7 NKJV

Maker of All Things, The
Jeremiah 51:19 NKJV

Maker of Earth Isaiah 45:18 MSG

Maker of Grain and Barley
Zechariah 10:1 MSG

Maker of Heaven 2 Kings 19:15 MSG

Man Accredited by God Acts 2:22 NIV

Man Attested by God, A Acts 2:22 NKJV

Manna Exodus 16:31 NKJV

Man of Sorrows, A Isaiah 53:3 NKJV

Man of War, A Exodus 15:3 NKJV

THE
AUTHORITATIVE
JESUS

Exploring the Wonders of Christ's Authority

> The glory which God had in the beginning, even the unapproachable glory of God, was also the Son's glory. The Father and the Son exist equally and are equally in power and possession.
>
> WATCHMAN NEE

TO SAY THAT CHRIST IS SUPREME in every way, as we suggested at the outset of this book, not only includes such definitions as "most excellent and highest in rank" but declares Christ to be "ultimate in power and authority." *Authority* is defined as

sions; jurisdiction." The most common New Testament Greek word for authority is *exousia*. It is sometimes translated as *power* and appears more than one hundred times in the New Testament.

control, superiority, mastery, predominance, reign, omnipotence." It is obvious from Scripture that Christ meets the standard for any definition one might give to the word *authority*.

We see, for example, reference to the supremacy of Christ's authority in these opening words from the author of the book of Hebrews:

> In the past God spoke to our ancestors through the prophets at many times and in various ways, but in these last days he has spoken to us by his Son, whom he appointed heir of all things, and through whom also he made the universe. The Son is the radiance of God's glory and the exact representation of his being, sustaining all things by his powerful word.
>
> HEBREWS 1:1–3 NIV

Authority and Relevance

Nothing validates the *Authoritative Jesus* more than to say He not only spoke the universe into existence, but sustains "all things by his powerful word." That clearly pictures supreme authority. Indeed, the very Bible itself, referred to as the Word of God, might be described as the Book of Jesus. It is also a book of both relevance and authority. Theologian John R. Stott would certainly agree: "The modern world detests authority but worships relevance. Our Christian conviction is that the Bible has both authority and relevance, and that the secret of both is Jesus Christ."[1]

John's gospel quotes multiple occasions when Christ Himself refers to the authority extended to Him from the Father. On one occasion, Christ had come to Jerusalem for one of the Jewish festivals. He was at the pool of Bethesda when He healed an invalid of 38 years. Because Christ had done this on the Sabbath, Jewish leaders began arguing with Him, intent on killing Him because He was even calling God His own Father and thus making Himself equal with God (John 5:16–18). Christ responded with one of His longest discourses recorded in the gospels. At one point, He says:

> "Most assuredly, I say to you, the hour is coming, and now is, when the dead will hear the voice of the Son of God; and those who hear will live. For as the Father has life in Himself, so He has granted the Son to have life in Himself, and has given Him authority to execute judgment also, because He is the Son of Man."
>
> JOHN 5:25–27 NKJV

It is clear when reviewing the various miracles that Christ performed, that in so doing He was validating his supreme authority given to Him by His Father. And in the same sense that Christ is supreme in all aspects of His character that we have examined thus far from the very beginning, which really had no beginning, to the very end, which really has no end, Christ will ever be the *Authoritative Jesus*! His authority is supreme and never ending.

The King of a Trillion Galaxies

Matthew describes a confrontation with Caiaphas, the high priest, along with members of the Sanhedrin, which again highlights the supremacy of His authority. Christ had been arrested and soon would be led to

dence against Christ so they could put Him to death. Finally, when two false witnesses obliged (Matthew 26:59–61), the high priest confronted Christ: "I demand in the name of the living God—tell us if you are the Messiah, the Son of God" (Matthew 26:63 NLT). Jesus replied, "You have said it. And in the future you will see the Son of Man seated in the place of power at God's right hand and coming on the clouds of heaven" (Matthew 26:64 NLT).

Bible scholars believe Christ was referencing Daniel's encounter when Daniel wrote:

> In my vision I saw one who looked like a son of man. He was com-
> ing with the clouds of heaven. He approached the Eternal God.
> He was led right up to him. And he was given authority, glory and
> a kingdom. People of all nations, no matter what language they
> spoke, worshiped him. His authority will last forever. It will not pass
> away. His kingdom will never be destroyed.
>
> DANIEL 7:13–14 NIRV

Christ was not only given authority by the Father, but it was an eternal, universal authority.

Clearly one of the most important statements regarding Christ's
authority came from His own lips when He commissioned His followers to go and disciple the nations. It is a familiar passage to many who
have been challenged by what the Church has long referred to as the
Great Commission. Most often, we quote the commission itself to "go
therefore and make disciples of all the nations" (Matthew 28:19 NKJV).
But we must not forget the words of Christ just before He commissioned
His disciples. Christ declared, "All authority has been given to Me in
heaven and on earth" (Matthew 28:18 NKJV).

There is no fence around the word *all*. *All* means "the whole extent or
quantity of a thing; everything, the whole thing that which represents
totality ! There is no "something else" or "a little bit more" beyond
all! The *Authoritative Jesus* has authority over *all*. His authority is
unconditional, unchallenged, unrestrained, unrestricted, absolute and
complete. He is the King of a trillion galaxies! His authority and reign
are universal. Jesus, indeed, is awesome! And here is the best part—He
wants to personally meet with you today. Don't miss that appointment.

THE
AUTHORITATIVE
JESUS

Exploring the Wonders of Christ's Authority

> The glory which God had in the beginning, even the unapproachable glory of God, was also the Son's glory. The Father and the Son exist equally and are equally in power and possession.
>
> WATCHMAN NEE

TO SAY THAT CHRIST IS SUPREME in every way, as we suggested at the outset of this book, not only includes such definitions as "most excellent and highest in rank" but declares Christ to be "ultimate in power and authority." *Authority* is defined as "the power or right to give commands, take action; make final decisions; jurisdiction." The most common New Testament Greek word for authority is *exousia*. It is sometimes translated as *power* and appears more than one hundred times in the New Testament.

A look at some of the synonyms for *authority* expands our understanding of how this word would apply to Christ: "command, dominion, control, superiority, mastery, predominance, reign, omnipotence." It is obvious from Scripture that Christ meets the standard for any definition one might give to the word *authority*.

We see, for example, reference to the supremacy of Christ's authority in these opening words from the author of the book of Hebrews:

> In the past God spoke to our ancestors through the prophets at many times and in various ways, but in these last days he has spoken to us by his Son, whom he appointed heir of all things, and through whom also he made the universe. The Son is the radiance of God's glory and the exact representation of his being, sustaining all things by his powerful word.
>
> HEBREWS 1:1–3 NIV

Authority and Relevance

Nothing validates the *Authoritative Jesus* more than to say He not only spoke the universe into existence, but sustains "all things by his powerful word." That clearly pictures supreme authority. Indeed, the very Bible itself, referred to as the Word of God, might be described as the Book of Jesus. It is also a book of both relevance and authority. Theologian John R. Stott would certainly agree: "The modern world detests authority but worships relevance. Our Christian conviction is that the Bible has both authority and relevance, and that the secret of both is Jesus Christ."[1]

John's gospel quotes multiple occasions when Christ Himself refers to the authority extended to Him from the Father. On one occasion, Christ had come to Jerusalem for one of the Jewish festivals. He was at the pool of Bethesda when He healed an invalid of 38 years. Because Christ had done this on the Sabbath, Jewish leaders began arguing with Him, intent on killing Him because He was even calling God His own Father and thus making Himself equal with God (John 5:16–18). Christ responded with one of His longest discourses recorded in the gospels. At one point, He says:

A PRAYER FOR TODAY

Jesus, all authority in heaven and on earth belongs to You! You hold authority over all creation, over all power, over eternity. I praise You today because Your authority brings healing, freedom and abundant life. I worship You because Your authority rules even over death. Jesus, I invite Your authority to reign in my life today. Search my heart and reveal to me any places where I have been resistant to Your authority. I want to bring every part of my heart, mind and soul into submission to Your authority. Your authority is always good, and it is the true desire of my heart. Amen.

Encountering the *Authoritative* Jesus:
A PRACTICAL APPLICATION

Remember—these four steps, as explained more fully on pages 23–24 in the introduction, are suggested to help you apply this quality of Christ to your own life.

1. **EXPLORE:** Take time to meditate on this quality of Christ. Use Scriptures in this chapter to get started.

2. **EXPERIENCE:** Turn your meditation into prayer that this quality might impact your life today. Pray the above prayer to begin.

3. **EXPRESS:** During your quiet time, take a moment to journal your thoughts, even if briefly.

4. **EXALT:** Pray, praise or even spontaneously sing your way through today's list of the names of Jesus. It only requires a few minutes.

GLORIFY HIS NAME

Praise be to his glorious *name* forever; may the whole
earth be filled with his glory. Amen and Amen.

PSALM 72:19 NIV, *emphasis added*

Man Who Suffered, A Isaiah 53:3 MSG

Master God, The Jeremiah 1:6 MSG

Master Jesus, The Revelation 22:20 MSG

Master of All Kings, The
Daniel 2:47 MSG

Master of All Masters
Deuteronomy 10:17 MSG

Master of Peace, The
2 Thessalonians 3:16 MSG

Master of the Earth, The
Micah 4:13 MSG

Master of the House, The
Luke 13:25 NLT

Mediator Job 9:33 NKJV

Mediator of a Better Covenant
Hebrews 8:6 NKJV

Mediator of the New Covenant
Hebrews 12:24 NKJV

Medicine in Gilead Jeremiah 8:22 NLT

Melchizedek Priest, The
Psalm 110:4 MSG

Merciful Father 2 Corinthians 1:3 NLT

Merciful God, A Deuteronomy 4:31 NIV

Mercy and Grace Psalm 103:8 MSG

Messenger of Good News, A
Isaiah 41:27 NIV

Messenger of the Covenant, The
Malachi 3:1 NLT

Messiah, The John 4:25–26 NLT

Messiah of God, The Luke 23:35 MSG

Mighty and Awesome
Deuteronomy 10:17 NIV

Mighty Lord, The Psalm 50:1 TPT

Mighty One of Israel, The
Isaiah 30:29 NKJV

Mighty Prophet, A Luke 7:16 NLT

Mighty Right Arm Isaiah 51:9 NLT

Mighty Rock Where I Hide
Psalm 94:22 NLT

Mighty Warrior Psalm 45:3 NLT

Minister of the Sanctuary, A
Hebrews 8:2 NKJV

THE
PRAYING
JESUS

Exploring the Wonders of Christ's Prayers

> Christ's life and work, His suffering and death—it was all prayer,
> all dependence on God, trust in God, receiving from God, sur-
> render to God.
>
> ANDREW MURRAY

AS MUCH AS ANY OTHER spiritual discipline that Christ
manifested in His time on earth, His prayer life would be
foundational. Everywhere Jesus walked, we could say He
prayer-walked! Christ was the embodiment of prayer. He was, quite
simply, the *Praying Jesus*.

Christ initiated His ministry, sustained His ministry and even concluded His ministry in prayer. He was always in a conversation with His
heavenly Father. And these were not mere moments of casual prayerful
reflections—a few words here, a few words there. Christ spent long hours
in the presence of His Father. We recall the words of Luke describing
the occasion of Christ choosing His disciples. Luke writes: "Now it
came to pass in those days that He went out to the mountain to pray,
and continued all night in prayer to God" (Luke 6:12 NKJV). Our youth
today would say, "Wow, Christ pulled an all-nighter!" Indeed, He spent
many all-nighters in the presence of His Father. Our Month in the Son

would clearly be incomplete without careful consideration of the *Praying Jesus.*

Solitary Places

Mark, writing in his gospel, describes another of those occasions when Christ, possibly exhausted from ministry the night before, slipped away to converse with His heavenly Father. Jesus had been ministering in the town of Capernaum. Earlier in the day, Jesus had been in the synagogue, and upon leaving with Andrew, James and John, He went to the house of Simon. Simon's mother-in-law lay sick with a fever, and Simon requested the prayers of Jesus. Christ took the woman's hand and lifted her up, and her fever immediately departed (Mark 1:30–31 NKJV).

Later that night, well after dark, a crowd gathered at the house where Jesus was still ministering. It was not a small gathering. Indeed, Mark records that "the whole city was gathered together at the door" (Mark 1:33 NKJV). It no doubt was a long night of ministry because Mark writes: "[Jesus] healed many who were sick with various diseases, and cast out many demons" (Mark 1:34 NKJV). I'm sure Christ had very little sleep because, as the text continues: "Now in the morning, having risen a long while before daylight, He went out and departed to a solitary place; and there He prayed" (Mark 1:35 NKJV).

Noteworthy in reading such passages is how Jesus, when no doubt exhausted from ministry, felt the need to retreat to a solitary place to spend time alone with His heavenly Father. Jesus clearly understood the significance of solitary places for prayerful restoration. Such was not only a discipline but a lifestyle. Christ likewise prayed faithfully for His disciples. His longest recorded prayer, John 17, is an example.

Here Christ prayed that God would protect His disciples by the power of His name so that "they may be one" (verse 11); He prayed that they may "have the full measure of my joy within them" (verse 13); He prayed that God would "protect them from the evil one" (verse 15); He prayed that God would "sanctify them" by the truth of His Word (verse 17); He prayed that they might be one "so that the world may believe that you have sent me" (verse 21); He prayed that they might be "brought to complete unity" so that the "world will know that you sent me" (verse 23); and He concludes by asking His Father that His disciples would see Christ's glory, "the glory you have given me because you loved me before the creation of the world" (verse 24 NIV). Jesus was a consummate leader. And He led by prayer.

Never Not Praying!

Interestingly, the prayer life of Jesus did not cease with His resurrection and ascension. He is still the *Praying Jesus*. Jesus is never not praying. The author of Hebrews reminds believers: "Therefore He is also able to save to the uttermost those who come to God through Him, since He always lives to make intercession for them" (Hebrews 7:25 NKJV).

One thing should become increasingly clear in our study of the awesome supremacy of Christ. If we desire to be like Jesus, we will ultimately be intercessors, because that is what Jesus is like. Intercession is His continuing heavenly ministry at the right hand of the Father. As we walk hand in hand with the *Praying Jesus*, it is understandable we will become praying people. How can it be otherwise? Thomas Goodwin, in *What Happens When I Pray?*, writes, "The person who knows Christ best is the person who will pray best."[1]

Have you spent time with the *Praying Jesus* today? Has it become a daily habit? We turn again to Oswald Chambers for both an affirming and a cautionary word: "When a man is born from above, the life of the Son of God begins in him, and he can either starve that life or nourish it. Prayer is the way the life of God is nourished. Our Lord nourished the life of God in Him by prayer. He was continually in contact with His Father."[2]

Have you sat alone with the *Praying Jesus* today? Have you seen through His eyes the possibilities of this day? Don't let the challenges before you, or the wisdom of the world, cloud your vision. Remember the words of Dwight L. Moody: "The Christian on his knees sees more than the philosopher on tiptoe."[3]

A PRAYER FOR TODAY

Today, O Lord, I thank You for Your glorious gift of prayer. Thank You for modeling a life of prayer. Thank You for showing me what it looks like to be a faithful intercessor, fully dependent on prayer as the substance of divine communion. Jesus, I long to meet You daily in the quiet place of prayer. I invite You to lead me in cultivating a sacred intimacy, resting in the wonder of Your presence. Draw me ever closer to Your heart and, by Your Spirit, help me grow in faithfulness to meet You there day by day. In this holy place, my heart rests before You, and in these moments, may I hear Your voice. Amen.

Encountering the *Praying* Jesus:
A PRACTICAL APPLICATION

Remember—these four steps, as explained more fully on pages 23–24 in the introduction, are suggested to help you apply this quality of Christ to your own life.

1. **EXPLORE:** Take time to meditate on this quality of Christ. Use Scriptures in this chapter to get started.

2. **EXPERIENCE:** Turn your meditation into prayer that this quality might impact your life today. Pray the above prayer to begin.

3. **EXPRESS:** During your quiet time, take a moment to journal your thoughts, even if briefly.

4. **EXALT:** Pray, praise or even spontaneously sing your way through today's list of the names of Jesus. It only requires a few minutes.

GLORIFY HIS NAME

———

Sing to God, sing praise to his *name*, extol him who rides on
the clouds—his *name* is the LORD—and rejoice before him.

PSALM 68:4 NIV1984, *emphasis added*

———

Miracle Sign, A Luke 2:34 TPT

Morning Light, The 2 Samuel 23:4 NLT

Morning Star, The 2 Peter 1:19 NLT

Morning without Clouds, A
2 Samuel 23:4 NKJV

Most Fierce Warrior, A
Jeremiah 20:11 MSG

Most High, The Psalm 18:13 NKJV

Most Holy, The Daniel 9:24 NKJV

Most Important Capstone of the
Arch Psalm 118:22 TPT

Most Jealous God, A Exodus 20:5 MSG

Most Wise God, A Isaiah 31:2 MSG

Mountain-Cliff Fortress Where I
Am Kept Safe Psalm 71:3 TPT

Mountain-Maker Psalm 65:6 MSG

Muzzler of Sea Storm Psalm 65:7 MSG

My Altar-Rock Psalm 19:14 MSG

My Bedrock Psalm 71:5 MSG

My Beloved Matthew 12:18 NKJV

My Best Friend Psalm 23:1 TPT

My Cave to Hide In Psalm 31:3 MSG

My Champion Isaiah 50:8 MSG

My Cliff to Climb Psalm 31:3 MSG

My Creator Job 35:10 NLT

My Elect One Isaiah 42:1 NKJV

My Entire Salvation 2 Samuel 23:5 MSG

My Every Desire 2 Samuel 23:5 MSG

My Exuberant God Psalm 43:4 MSG

My Faithful God Psalm 31:5 NIV

My Free and Freeing God
Psalm 18:46 MSG

My Friend Song of Solomon 5:16 NLT

My Glory Psalm 3:3 NKJV

THE
FAITHFUL
JESUS

Exploring the Wonders of Christ's Faithfulness

> All God's giants have been weak men and women who have gotten hold of God's faithfulness.
>
> HUDSON TAYLOR

GOD CANNOT CHANGE," writes Graham Cooke. "He cannot be anything other than who He is. Out of His love and His promises, you were selected as His treasure. God's faithfulness has been the bedrock of His dealings with humanity throughout time."[1]

Our Month in the Son journey to explore the wonders of Christ's nature brings us to what Graham Cooke refers to as "the bedrock of His dealings with humanity throughout time." We come to engage our thoughts on the awesome wonders of the *Faithful Jesus*.

Faithful is defined as "steadfast in allegiance; firm in adherences to keeping promises or in observance of duty; true to the facts." *Faithful* comes from the Middle English word *feith*, meaning "faith" and "ful," or "having in it all there is space for" (e.g, "full of faith").

Forever Faithful

Scripture is filled with promises of our Lord's faithfulness. Paul wrote this affirmation to the Corinthian believers:

> Therefore you do not lack any spiritual gift as you eagerly wait for our Lord Jesus Christ to be revealed. He will also keep you firm to the end, so that you will be blameless on the day of our Lord Jesus Christ. God is faithful, who has called you into fellowship with his Son, Jesus Christ our Lord.
>
> 1 Corinthians 1:7–9 NIV

The apostle wrote to Timothy, saying, "This is a faithful saying: For if we died with Him, we shall also live with Him. If we endure, we shall also reign with Him. If we deny Him, He also will deny us. If we are faithless, He remains faithful; He cannot deny Himself" (2 Timothy 2:11–13 NKJV). Indeed, Christ is forever faithful!

Paul further amplifies this promise of God's faithfulness in his first letter to the Thessalonian believers. As he concludes, he admonishes believers to "test all things; hold fast what is good. Abstain from every form of evil" (1 Thessalonians 5:21–22 NKJV). Then the apostle offers both a prayer and a promise: "Now may the God of peace Himself sanctify you completely; and may your whole spirit, soul, and body be preserved blameless at the coming of our Lord Jesus Christ. He who calls you is faithful, who also will do it" (1 Thessalonians 5:23–24 NKJV).

It is often during seasons of suffering, experiencing loss or facing unusual and unexpected hardships that it is easy to question the Lord's faithfulness. The apostle Peter reminds us, "Therefore let those who suffer according to the will of God commit their souls to Him in doing good, as to a faithful Creator" (1 Peter 4:19 NKJV). David Wilkerson, author of the widely read classic *The Cross and the Switchblade*, spoke of how these difficult spiritual tests reveal God's faithfulness: "Our faith is not meant to get us out of a hard place or change our painful condition. Rather, it is meant to reveal God's faithfulness to us in the midst of our dire situation."[2]

There are occasions in life when we may suffer the loss of things very dear to us. The pain of that loss may at times be almost unbearable. Sometimes God uses these circumstances to help us loosen our grip on things we need to release in order for God to fulfill His purposes in our lives. I recall the words of Martin Luther: "I have held many things in my hands, and I have lost them all; but whatever I have placed in God's hands that I still possess."[3]

A Pen That Never Blots

Four decades ago, as my daily prayer life continued to grow, I decided to begin journaling a summary of my daily encounters in prayer. I shared about this briefly in the introduction to this book. Recently I celebrated my fortieth year of keeping that daily record. These writings are now in 31 volumes (small, three-ring binders) that I keep on two shelves in my prayer room at home. Of course, every day I'm adding new pages to those binders.

Over the years, when I was feeling discouraged or facing difficulties that seemed unsurmountable, I sometimes reached up toward one of the shelves containing my journals and randomly pulled one down. Again, at random I would open that journal and begin to read some of the daily entries. I cannot recall a single instance of doing this that did not result in tears as I reflected back on how God led my wife and me through some particular season or how God had miraculously met a need. New faith would always come.

On one of those occasions, I was reminded of a passage in Revelation that speaks of God's saints overcoming our enemy, who is defined as the "accuser of our brethren" (Revelation 12:10). In that passage of Scripture, it tells how the enemy is overcome by two things: "the blood of the Lamb and . . . the word of their testimony" (Revelation 12:11 NKJV). Of course, the reference to "the word of their testimony" could refer to the written record of Scripture of God's saints overcoming the many assaults of Satan. But I believe it also relates to the testimony of ordinary believers who see how God has sustained them through their many tests and trials.

What a joy it is for me to daily take into my hands the Word of God and know that it is a Book of Promises with God's faithfulness written on page after page! Dwight L. Moody was correct: "God never made a promise that was too good to be true!" Charles Spurgeon adds with his usual wit, "God writes with a pen that never blots, speaks with a tongue that never slips, acts with a hand that never fails."[4] To walk daily with the *Faithful Jesus* is to walk into each new day with a confidence that no matter the challenges we may face along life's journey, just having Jesus walking beside us is the answer to any prayer we could ever pray.

A PRAYER FOR TODAY

Faithful Jesus, holy and true, I bow before You today in deep gratitude. As I read about Your faithfulness, I call to mind all the ways You have shown Yourself faithful to me. I think over the time I have walked with You, and I remember all the ways—big and small—You have been faithful. You have been faithful to Your Word, faithful to Your promises, and faithful to be present to me at all times. Thank You, Jesus. I pray that I would grow in walking in the truth of Your faithfulness. May my heart rest before You, always trusting You will be faithful. Amen.

Encountering the *Faithful* Jesus:
A PRACTICAL APPLICATION

Remember—these four steps, as explained more fully on pages 23–24 in the introduction, are suggested to help you apply this quality of Christ to your own life.

1. **EXPLORE:** Take time to meditate on this quality of Christ. Use Scriptures in this chapter to get started.

2. **EXPERIENCE:** Turn your meditation into prayer that this quality might impact your life today. Pray the above prayer to begin.

3. **EXPRESS:** During your quiet time, take a moment to journal your thoughts, even if briefly.

4. **EXALT:** Pray, praise or even spontaneously sing your way through today's list of the names of Jesus. It only requires a few minutes.

GLORIFY HIS NAME

Help us, O God our Savior, for the glory of your *name*;
deliver us and forgive our sins for your *name's* sake.

PSALM 79:9 NIV1984, *emphasis added*

My **Helper** Psalm 115:11 NLT

My **Hero** Psalm 62:7 TPT

My **Hideout** Psalm 94:22 TPT

My **High Mountain Retreat**
Psalm 94:22 MSG

My **High Tower** Psalm 144:2 NKJV

My **Island Hideaway** Psalm 32:7 MSG

My **King from the Very Start**
Psalm 74:12 MSG

My **King of Righteousness**
Psalm 110:4 TPT

My **Lamp** 2 Samuel 22:29 NLT

My **Light** Psalm 27:1 NLT

My **Lord and My God** John 20:28 NKJV

My **Lover** Song of Solomon 2:16 NLT

My **Loving God** Psalm 144:2 NIV

My **Maker** Job 35:10 NKJV

My **Master** John 20:28 MSG

My **Mighty Rock** Psalm 62:7 NIV

My **Mountain of Strength**
Psalm 42:9 TPT

My **Place of Quiet Retreat**
Psalm 119:114 MSG

My **Portion** Psalm 73:26; 119:57 NKJV

My **Power** 2 Samuel 22:33 NKJV

My **Protector-God** Psalm 19:14 TPT

My **Redeemer** Psalm 19:14 NLT

My **Revelation-Light** Psalm 27:1 TPT

My **Righteous Servant** Isaiah 53:11 NKJV

My **Rock and My Fortress**
Psalm 31:3 NIV

My **Rock of Protection** Psalm 31:2 NLT

My **Rock of Refuge** Psalm 31:2 NKJV

My **Rock-Solid God** Psalm 42:9 MSG

THE
MIRACULOUS
JESUS

Exploring the Wonders of Christ's Miracles

Jesus' miracles are not just a challenge to our minds, but a promise to our hearts, that the world we want is coming.

TIM KELLER

BASILEA SCHLINK might well be described as the Mystic Mother of the twentieth century. She had an especially deep impact on my prayer life through her writings during my early ministry. Mother Basilea, as she was known by her fellow sisters, was a cofounder of the Evangelical Sisterhood of Mary in Darmstadt, Germany, in 1947. She led the order until her death in 2001. I borrow her timeless words as we continue our Month in the Son to help introduce to you the *Miraculous Jesus*:

> When human reason has exhausted every possibility, the children can go to their Father and receive all they need. . . . For only when you have become utterly dependent upon prayer and faith, only when all human possibilities have been exhausted, can you begin to reckon that God will intervene and work His miracles.[1]

Jesus represents the very hands of God reaching out to hurting humanity to work His miracles. The word *miracle* is generally defined as "an event or action that apparently contradicts known scientific laws and is hence thought to be due to supernatural causes, especially to an act of God." It is also defined as "a remarkable event or thing; a marvel."

The Miraculous Messiah

The miracles of Jesus, in my opinion, are first and foremost to validate that Christ is the "sent one," or the Messiah. Many of Christ's miracles, of course, involved healing the sick or delivering the demon possessed. Matthew records:

> Jesus traveled throughout the region of Galilee, teaching in the synagogues and announcing the Good News about the Kingdom. And he healed every kind of disease and illness. News about him spread as far as Syria, and people soon began bringing to him all who were sick. And whatever their sickness or disease, or if they were demon possessed or epileptic or paralyzed—he healed them all. Large crowds followed him wherever he went.
>
> MATTHEW 4:23–25 NLT

Christ's miracles were not confined only to the natural order, but they extended to the supernatural order as well. In His divinity before coming to earth in His incarnation, Christ's very words created the universe (Hebrews 1:1–4). We highlighted this in an earlier chapter on the *Creative Jesus*. It is therefore not difficult to understand that Christ had authority over the very universe He had created when He commanded the winds to cease on a stormy Galilean sea. Matthew writes:

> Suddenly a furious storm came up on the lake, so that the waves swept over the boat. But Jesus was sleeping. The disciples went and woke him, saying, "Lord, save us! We're going to drown!" He

replied, "You of little faith, why are you so afraid?" Then he got up and rebuked the winds and the waves, and it was completely calm. The men were amazed and asked, "What kind of man is this? Even the winds and the waves obey him!"

MATTHEW 8:24–27 NIV

Healing the Human Spirit

Our *Miraculous Jesus* not only healed the sick, but He healed the human spirit as well.

[Jesus] went all over Galilee. He used synagogues for meeting places and taught people the truth of God. God's kingdom was his theme—that beginning right now they were under God's government, a good government! He also healed people of their diseases and of the bad effects of their bad lives. Word got around the entire Roman province of Syria. People brought anybody with an ailment, whether mental, emotional, or physical. Jesus healed them, one and all.

MATTHEW 4:23–25 MSG

When Peter first preached the Gospel to the Gentiles who had gathered at the house of Cornelius, he explained:

This is the message of Good News for the people of Israel—that there is peace with God through Jesus Christ, who is Lord of all. . . . And you know that God anointed Jesus of Nazareth with the Holy Spirit and with power. Then Jesus went around doing good and healing all who were oppressed by the devil, for God was with him.

ACTS 10:36, 38 NLT

Note the expression "healing all who were oppressed by the devil." The word *oppressed* means "to weigh heavily on the mind, spirits, or senses; to cause worry or trouble." A further definition reads, "To keep down by the cruel or unjust use of power or authority." This speaks of the attempts of Satan to destroy the human spirit. The very presence of the *Miraculous Jesus* overcomes that oppression. In that sense, the mere presence of Christ is, in and of itself, the miracle.

I worked with a leader who once shared with me details of his life before experiencing his conversion to Christ. He explained how radically different he had become in a matter of moments when Christ came into his life. His brain, he told me, was transformed overnight. He mentioned that over the years since his conversion he had heard several testimonies of believers who had been miraculously healed and who sometimes would show X-rays from doctors revealing how a sizable tumor or some other abnormality appeared when an initial X-ray was taken, but later when a second X-ray was taken just prior to surgery, the tumor or abnormality had completely disappeared. My friend said he wished someone could have taken an X-ray of his brain before his conversion, and then another after. He explained that anyone who compared the two X-rays would have said it was as great a miracle as any they had ever seen. That miracle, in a word, was *Jesus*.

You, too, if Christ is in you, are a living miracle. If you are yet to know Christ personally, and you willingly welcome Him into your life, as did my friend, the same can happen to you, in an instant. The change is only a prayer away. And best of all, together we can step into each new day knowing that the *Miraculous Jesus* is walking beside us each step of the way.

A PRAYER FOR TODAY

Jesus, I bow before You today in awe of Your healing power and matchless miracles. The stories of Your miraculous life reveal to me Your caring heart for a hurting world. I see Your power in bringing life to the lifeless and setting captives free. In these moments in Your presence, I prayerfully invite Your miraculous power into my everyday circumstances. Thank You for meeting me daily in my areas of anxiety, weakness and need. May Your Kingdom purposes reign in my health, in my life, in my work, in my relationships and in my world. And for the greatest miracle of my life, just knowing You, I gratefully thank You. Amen.

Encountering the *Miraculous* Jesus:
A PRACTICAL APPLICATION

Remember—these four steps, as explained more fully on pages 23–24 in the introduction, are suggested to help you apply this quality of Christ to your own life.

1. **EXPLORE:** Take time to meditate on this quality of Christ. Use Scriptures in this chapter to get started.

2. **EXPERIENCE:** Turn your meditation into prayer that this quality might impact your life today. Pray the above prayer to begin.

3. **EXPRESS:** During your quiet time, take a moment to journal your thoughts, even if briefly.

4. **EXALT:** Pray, praise or even spontaneously sing your way through today's list of the names of Jesus. It only requires a few minutes.

GLORIFY HIS NAME

All the nations you have made will come and worship
before you, O Lord; they will bring glory to your *name*.

Psalm 86:9 NIV1984, *emphasis added*

My Safe Leader Psalm 31:3 MSG

My Safe Place Psalm 94:22 TPT

My Safe Retreat When Trouble
Descends Jeremiah 16:19 MSG

My Salvation Psalm 38:22 NKJV

My Salvation God Psalm 51:14 MSG

My Savior-God Psalm 18:46 TPT

My Servant Isaiah 42:1 NLT

My Shepherd Psalm 23:1 NKJV

My Shield 2 Samuel 22:3 NKJV

My Song Isaiah 12:2 NKJV

My Soul's True Love
Song of Solomon 3:2 TPT

My Strength 2 Samuel 22:3 NKJV

My Strength and My Song
Isaiah 12:2 NLT

My Strong Champion Psalm 118:7 MSG

My Stronghold Psalm 18:2 NIV

My Stronghold of Salvation
Psalm 31:3 TPT

My Strong Shelter and Hiding
Place on High Psalm 31:2 TPT

My Support Psalm 18:18 NLT

My True Mountain Guide
Psalm 31:3 MSG

My True Shelter Psalm 94:22 TPT

My True Strength Psalm 118:14 TPT

My True Tower of Strength
Psalm 94:22 TPT

My Well-Beloved Isaiah 5:1 NKJV

My Witness Job 16:19 NIV

Nail into a Solid Wall, A
Isaiah 22:23 MSG

Nazarene, A Matthew 2:23 MSG

Near One, The Psalm 75:1 TPT

THE
WORTHY
JESUS

Exploring the Wonders of Christ's Worthiness

> If you had a thousand crowns you should put them all on the
> head of Christ! And if you had a thousand tongues they should
> all sing his praise, for he is worthy.
>
> WILLIAM TIPTAFT

"CHRIST IS NOT VALUED AT ALL unless He be valued above all."[1] These powerful words from the pen of early Church father Augustine of Hippo bring our Month in the Son journey to worship at the feet of the *Worthy Jesus*.

Our word *worship* is derived from the Old English word *weorthscipe*, which means "to ascribe worth, to pay homage, to reverence or to venerate." Worship focuses on the importance of worth or worthiness. In ancient times *weorthscipe* literally meant "worthness."[2]

Nathan Bierma, of Calvin Theological Seminary, explains:

> The root word of "worship" can also help remind us what worship is meant to be. Worship, or "worth-ship," is an act of affirming God's worth—not boosting God's self-esteem, not mere deference or flattery, and not appeasement. . . . But worship is, fundamentally, a declaration that God is worthy.[3]

We see a picture of this kind of worship in Revelation 5, when the elders and living creatures, holding harps for worship and golden bowls full of the prayers of the saints, come before the throne of God saying, "Worthy is the Lamb, who was slain, to receive power and wealth and wisdom and strength and honor and glory and praise!" (Revelation 5:12 NIV).

A chapter earlier in Christ's revelation to John, the apostle writes, "You are worthy, O Lord our God, to receive glory and honor and power. For you created all things, and they exist because you created what you pleased" (Revelation 4:11 NLT).

The author of Hebrews adds his voice to our discussion:

> Therefore, holy brethren, partakers of a heavenly calling, consider Jesus, the Apostle and High Priest of our confession; He was faithful to Him who appointed Him, as Moses also was in all His house. For He has been counted worthy of more glory than Moses, by just so much as the builder of the house has more honor than the house.
>
> HEBREWS 3:1–3 NASB

A Visible Habitation of God

One of the greatest missionary movements in history began because a band of persecuted believers focused on the worthiness of Jesus. It all began with a wealthy nobleman, Nikolaus Ludwig von Zinzendorf, in the early 1700s. Zinzendorf grew up in a religious family that became Lutherans during the Reformation. Spiritually sensitive even as a child of just six, young Nikolaus would often write love letters to Jesus, climb to the castle tower, and toss them out the window. It was a precursor to how Zinzendorf would be used of the Lord to ignite one of the great missionary enterprises in history. And it would happen during one of the most difficult eras for missionaries to be sent to the ends of the earth, the 1700s.

Zinzendorf owned a large estate in Saxony (modern Germany). He named it Herrnhut, meaning "watch of the Lord." Herrnhut, founded in 1722, soon became home to several hundred persecuted Christians from Bohemia and Moravia. For the first five years of Herrnhut, the community hardly lived up to its name. Dissension and hostility permeated the atmosphere. Finally, in early 1727, Zinzendorf and several others, including the leader of the persecuted believers, agreed together to seek God earnestly for revival.

That revival came gloriously and suddenly on May 12, 1727. The entire community was transformed. Later Zinzendorf would write in his journals, "The whole place represented truly a visible habitation of God among men."[4] Soon Zinzendorf and others organized a prayer watch that initially included 24 men and 24 women. They covenanted together to each spend one hour a day in prayer, at different times, so as to cover all 24 hours daily in prayer. It was to begin a prayer watch that would continue unbroken for more than one hundred years.

Celebrate His Worthiness

The result of a century of continuous prayer was the birth of a mission's movement unprecedented for that season in human history. To become known as the Moravian Missions Movement, the missionary enterprise began in 1731, when Count Zinzendorf met a black slave from St. Thomas Island in the West Indies. This greatly impacted the count, who shared his burden with the whole community. As a result, two men volunteered to sail to St. Thomas to reach slaves with the Gospel. Soon others followed, including some who would literally sell themselves into slavery in order to ultimately reach slaves who needed Jesus.

Although many Church historians would later refer to William Carey as the father of modern missions, it is noteworthy that sixty years before Carey sailed for India, the Moravians had already sent out over three hundred missionaries to the ends of the earth. Over the following 150 years, the Moravians would commission 2,158 foreign missionaries, an unprecedented number for that era in history.

From the very first missionaries being sent out, a motto emerged that would forever be identified with Moravian missions. It is said that when the two initial missionaries were preparing to sail, friends and loved ones who had traveled to see them off began to weep as they waved good-bye. The men shouted in response, "The Lamb is worthy to receive the reward of His sufferings!" In the following century, that response would be heard hundreds of times.

The Lamb is, indeed, worthy—worthy enough that we would set apart a sacred moment every day just to sit with our Lord, listen to His Word and celebrate His worthiness.

A PRAYER FOR TODAY

Worthy Jesus, Lamb of God! Lord, You are worthy of all my honor and praise. You are worthy to be worshiped night and day. You are worthy of my living sacrifice. Jesus, I focus my heart and mind on Your worthiness today. I am overwhelmed by all You are and all You have done. I am overcome by the desire to worship You. I long to give You everything, Jesus. I pray that my life would reflect my deep and thorough belief in Your worthiness. May every part of me be ordered around You. I submit everything to You in reverence, Lord Jesus. Amen.

Encountering the *Worthy* Jesus:
A PRACTICAL APPLICATION

Remember—these four steps, as explained more fully on pages 23–24 in the introduction, are suggested to help you apply this quality of Christ to your own life.

1. **EXPLORE:** Take time to meditate on this quality of Christ. Use Scriptures in this chapter to get started.

2. **EXPERIENCE:** Turn your meditation into prayer that this quality might impact your life today. Pray the above prayer to begin.

3. **EXPRESS:** During your quiet time, take a moment to journal your thoughts, even if briefly.

4. **EXALT:** Pray, praise or even spontaneously sing your way through today's list of the names of Jesus. It only requires a few minutes.

GLORIFY HIS NAME

I will praise God's *name* in song and
glorify him with thanksgiving.

PSALM 69:30 NIV, *emphasis added*

Not a God Far Off Jeremiah 23:23 MSG

Ocean-Pourer Psalm 65:6 MSG

Offering, An Ephesians 5:2 NKJV

Offering for Sin, An Isaiah 53:10 MSG

Ointment Poured Forth
Song of Solomon 1:3 NKJV

One and Only, The Psalm 62:1 MSG

One and Only God of Wonders
Psalm 72:18 TPT

One and Only God Who Delivers,
The Hosea 13:4 MSG

One and Only High God on Earth,
The Psalm 83:18 MSG

One and Only Son John 3:16 NLT

One Comforting You, The
Isaiah 51:12 MSG

One Enthroned in Heaven
Psalm 2:4 NIV

One for Whom We Wait, The
Jeremiah 14:22 MSG

One from East to West, The
Psalm 75:6 MSG

One I Love, The
Song of Solomon 3:2 NKJV

One Living Forever and Ever, The
Revelation 10:6 MSG

One My Heart Loves
Song of Solomon 3:2 NIV

One-of-a-Kind God-Expression
John 1:18 MSG

One-of-a-Kind Son of God, The
John 3:18 MSG

One of Glory, The Zechariah 2:8 MSG

One Shepherd John 10:16 NKJV

One Who Answers and Satisfies,
The Hosea 14:8 MSG

One Who Armed You for This
Work, The Isaiah 45:5 MSG

One Who Can Be Trusted
Romans 10:14 MSG

One Who Delivered You from
Egypt Amos 2:10 MSG

One Who Guarantees, The
Hebrews 7:22 NLT

One Who Is Appearing
Hebrews 10:37 TPT

One Who Lifts My Head High
Psalm 3:3 NIV

THE
RIGHTEOUS
JESUS

Exploring the Wonders of Christ's Righteousness

> There is in Jesus Christ more merit and righteousness than the whole world has need of.
>
> JOHN BUNYAN

JOHN BUNYAN'S CLASSIC MASTERPIECE *The Pilgrim's Progress* has touched believers over multiple generations since its first edition in 1678. It is one of the most published works in the English language. By 1938, 250 years after Bunyan's death, already 1,300 editions of the book had been printed. A prolific writer for his generation, Bunyan's legacy includes 58 published titles. In his autobiography, *Grace Abounding to the Chief of Sinners*, a testimony of his spiritual journey, Bunyan introduces us to our next view of the nature of Christ—the *Righteous Jesus*:

> Christ was all—all my righteousness, all my sanctification, and all my redemption. . . . Moreover, the Lord also led me into the mystery of union with the Son of God, and I saw that I was joined to Him, that I was flesh of His flesh and bone of His bone. And if He and I were one, then His righteousness was mine, His merits mine, His

victory also mine. Now I could see myself in heaven and earth at the same time; in heaven by my Christ, my Head, my righteousness, and my life; and on earth by my own body.[1]

In a single verse of Scripture, the apostle Paul sums up the essence of Christ's righteousness: "God made [Christ] who had no sin to be sin for us, so that in him we might become the righteousness of God" (2 Corinthians 5:21 NIV). *Righteousness* is simply defined as: "acting in a just, upright manner; morally right, fair and just; moral excellence or perfection." Of course, when speaking of Christ's righteousness, we are, indeed, speaking of righteousness to the supreme. Our Month in the Son would be incomplete without a special encounter with the *Righteous Jesus.*

Paul further explained in his letter to Christians at Rome that in believing in Christ, His righteousness becomes our righteousness because of Christ's sacrifice on the cross. He wrote:

> God sacrificed Jesus on the altar of the world to clear that world of sin. Having faith in him sets us in the clear. God decided on this course of action . . . to set the world in the clear with himself through the sacrifice of Jesus, finally taking care of the sins he had so patiently endured. . . . God sets things right. He also makes it possible for us to live in his rightness.
>
> ROMANS 3:25–26 MSG

The Fruit of Righteousness

Rightness is a good synonym for *righteousness. Rightness* is defined as: "the state or quality of being in accordance with what is just, good, or proper." It is also "conforming to facts or truth." Only the *Righteous Jesus* can make us righteous in the eyes of God.

The apostle Paul prayed earnestly for all those in his sphere of influence, that righteousness would be a fruit resulting from their continuing relationship with the *Righteous Jesus*. To the believers at Philippi, Paul wrote about his prayers on their behalf:

> God can testify how I long for all of you with the affection of Christ Jesus. And this is my prayer: that your love may abound more and more in knowledge and depth of insight, so that you may be able to discern what is best and may be pure and blameless for the day of Christ, filled with the fruit of righteousness that comes through Jesus Christ—to the glory and praise of God.
>
> Philippians 1:8–11 NIV

When Paul spoke here of his prayers for these believers, that they might "discern what is best and may be pure and blameless," he was speaking of that "rightness" we highlighted moments ago. He also made it clear that the "fruit of righteousness" only comes through Christ. Righteousness, as is the case with holiness, is not keeping lists of certain things we can or cannot do, but it is simply drawing from Christ's presence within us, so that in being like Him, the list of do's and don'ts is not needed.

No Ordinary Crown

Although maintaining some kind of list of do's and don'ts is not a good picture of biblical righteousness, the pursuit of righteousness ought to be a goal. Paul admonished young Timothy, "Pursue righteousness and a godly life, along with faith, love, perseverance, and gentleness" (1 Timothy 6:11 NLT). In examining these words of Paul to Timothy more carefully, it seems the pursuit of righteousness and a godly life is what would naturally be accompanied with (or even resulting in) the other qualities Paul mentions, including "faith, love, perseverance, and gentleness." If Christ is our righteousness, it would seem the more of Christ we have, the more righteousness we will receive. But one thing is certain—all our righteousness is in Christ.

When the apostle Paul realized his life was drawing to a close, he told his treasured companion, Timothy, that his life had been "poured out as an offering to God" (2 Timothy 4:6 NLT). He then told Timothy, "And now the prize awaits me—the crown of righteousness, which the Lord, the righteous Judge, will give me on the day of his return. And the prize is not just for me but for all who eagerly look forward to his appearing" (2 Timothy 4:8 NLT).

It is not without significance that a crown, which represents "position, power, or dominion of a monarch," was awaiting the apostle Paul, as well as all of God's children who eagerly await Christ's return. It is also noteworthy that in Christ's revelation to John, all those who are victorious and obey Christ "to the very end" (Revelation 2:26 NLT) will "rule the nations" and will have, as Christ clearly promises, "the same authority I received from my Father" (Revelation 2:27-28 NLT). This is no ordinary crown. If we take these words literally, and we should, as righteous people serving a righteous Lord, we will one day rule the universe with the *Righteous Jesus*.

A PRAYER FOR TODAY

Lord Jesus, I come into the place of prayer before You today with my soul focused on Your righteousness. I thank You for Your righteousness, Jesus. I grow more and more deeply aware of the high price Your righteousness paid for my eternal salvation. I long for the day when I will wear Your righteousness like a crown. Lord, I pray that my life would be totally transformed in light of Your righteousness. As I am clothed in Your righteousness, may every part of me become more like You. Amen.

Encountering the *Righteous* Jesus:
A PRACTICAL APPLICATION

Remember—these four steps, as explained more fully on pages 23–24 in the introduction, are suggested to help you apply this quality of Christ to your own life.

1. **EXPLORE:** Take time to meditate on this quality of Christ. Use Scriptures in this chapter to get started.

2. **EXPERIENCE:** Turn your meditation into prayer that this quality might impact your life today. Pray the above prayer to begin.

3. **EXPRESS:** During your quiet time, take a moment to journal your thoughts, even if briefly.

4. **EXALT:** Pray, praise or even spontaneously sing your way through today's list of the names of Jesus. It only requires a few minutes.

GLORIFY HIS NAME

I will praise you, O Lord my God, with all my
heart; I will glorify your *name* forever.

<small>PSALM 86:12 NIV1984,</small> *emphasis added*

One Who Made the Earth, The
Jeremiah 27:5 MSG

**One Who Represents Mortals
before God** Job 16:21 MSG

One Who Rescues, The
Romans 11:26 NLT

One Who Rules in Heaven
Psalm 2:4 NLT

One Who Shall Have Dominion
Numbers 24:19 NKJV

**One Who Takes Care of Your Sins,
The** Isaiah 43:25 MSG

**One Who Watches Our Every
Move, The** Psalm 76:11 MSG

One Who's on Your Side, The
Isaiah 49:25 MSG

One Whom God Sent, The
John 3:34 MSG

One You So Cruelly Abandoned
Isaiah 31:6 MSG

One You've Been Waiting For, The
Malachi 3:1 MSG

Only Begotten of the Father, The
John 1:14 NKJV

Only God There Is, The
Isaiah 45:5–6 MSG

**Only God Who Does Things Right,
The** Isaiah 45:21 MSG

**Only God Who Is Worthy of
the Highest Honors, The**
1 Timothy 1:17 TPT

**Only Most High God Exalted over
All the Earth, The** Psalm 83:18 TPT

Only Powerful One 1 Timothy 6:15 TPT

Only Real God, The Hosea 13:4 MSG

Only Savior There Is, The
Isaiah 43:11 MSG

Only True Hero, The Psalm 115:9–11 TPT

Only Wise God, The 1 Timothy 1:17 KJV

Our Favorite Word Psalm 75:1 MSG

Our Glorious God Acts 7:2 NLT

Our Great God Titus 2:13 NKJV

Our Hope 1 Timothy 1:1 NKJV

Our Lawgiver Isaiah 33:22 NKJV

Our Life-Giver 1 Timothy 1:1 TPT

Our Living Hope 1 Timothy 1:1 MSG

THE
SELFLESS
JESUS

Exploring the Wonders of Christ's Selflessness

The measure of a man's greatness is not the number of servants
he has, but the number of people he serves.

JOHN HAGEE

O UR MONTH IN THE SON INVITES US today to set aside
sacred moments to encounter the *Selfless Jesus*. As much as
any other quality that one might ascribe to Christ during His
earthly ministry was His selfless, servant lifestyle. *Selfless* is defined
as: "devoted to the welfare of other interests and not one's own; unself-
ish, altruistic, showing or prompted by unselfishness; self-sacrificing."
Christ was the embodiment of selflessness. He lived to serve. Paul would
especially highlight this quality when he wrote Philippian believers,
admonishing them to embrace the mind of Christ:

> Think of yourselves the way Christ Jesus thought of himself. . . .
> He lived a selfless, obedient life and then died a selfless, obedient
> death—and the worst kind of death at that—a crucifixion. Because
> of that obedience, God lifted him high and honored him far beyond
> anyone or anything, ever, so that all created beings in heaven and

on earth—even those long ago dead and buried—will bow in worship before this Jesus Christ.

PHILIPPIANS 2:5, 8–10 MSG

To Stand Out, Step Down!

We recall the occasion when Jesus had been ministering with His disciples in Galilee and throughout the region of Judea and now began to head toward Jerusalem. Jesus made it clear that it would be in Jerusalem that He would be betrayed and sentenced to death (Matthew 20:18).

After Christ explained to His disciples that on the third day following His death, He would be raised alive, the mother of James and John seized the opportunity to appeal to Jesus on behalf of her sons. She pleaded, "Give your word that these two sons of mine will be awarded the highest places of honor in your kingdom, one at your right hand, one at your left hand" (Matthew 20:21 MSG). When the other disciples heard this, they were indignant. Jesus then sought to settle them down, and in the process, He painted a picture of what it means to live a selfless life. He explained:

> Whoever wants to be great must become a servant. Whoever wants to be first among you must be your slave. That is what the Son of Man has done: He came to serve, not be served—and then to give away his life in exchange for the many who are held hostage.

MATTHEW 20:27–28 MSG

Later, after arriving in Jerusalem and only days before facing the cross, Jesus again touched on the subject of the selfless lifestyle. He spoke about the hypocrisy of religious scholars to His disciples, as well as to a crowd that had gathered, including the Pharisees (Matthew 23:1–7). Our Lord explained how these religious scholars burdened their students with lengthy lists of rules and demands while they themselves loved to "sit at the head table at church dinners, basking in the most prominent positions" (Matthew 23:6 MSG). The Lord then cautioned His listeners, "Don't let people do that to you, put you on a pedestal like that. . . . Do you want to stand out? Then step down. Be a servant" (Matthew 23:8, 11 MSG).

In many ways, such a servant lifestyle is both a calling and a gift. Peter wrote, "God has given each of you a gift from his great variety of spiritual gifts. Use them well to serve one another" (1 Peter 4:10 NLT).

Basins and Towels

Other gospel writers also highlighted Christ's instructions on living the life of a servant. Mark records: "[Jesus] sat down and summoned the Twelve. 'So you want first place? Then take the last place. Be the servant of all'" (Mark 9:35 MSG). John echoes these same sentiments of Christ: "If any of you wants to serve me, then follow me. Then you'll be where I am, ready to serve at a moment's notice. The Father will honor and reward anyone who serves me" (John 12:26 MSG). Luke, too, highlighted this same servant quality when he recorded these words of Jesus: "To you who are ready for the truth, I say this: Love your enemies. Let them bring out the best in you, not the worst. . . . If someone takes unfair advantage of you, use the occasion to practice the servant life. . . . Live generously" (Luke 6:27–30 MSG).

Christ Himself provided His disciples with an illustrated sermon on a servant lifestyle when He washed their feet (John 13:1–17). He concluded His feet-washing servant-act by asking His disciples a question: "Do you understand what I have done to you?" (John 13:12b, MSG). He then answered His own question: "I've laid down a pattern for you. What I've done, you do" (John 13:15 MSG). Charles Spurgeon, speaking on this passage, suggested Christ has never stopped serving:

> The Lord Jesus loves His people so much that, every day, He is still doing for them much that is analogous to wash their soiled feet. He accepts their poorest actions, feels their deepest sorrows, hears their slenderest wishes, and forgives all their transgressions. He is still their Servant, as well as their Friend and Master. He not only performs majestic deeds for them as their High Priest. . . . He also humbly and patiently goes among His people with basin and towel.[1]

Are you ready to walk daily beside the *Selfless Jesus*? If your answer is yes, don't forget your basin and towel!

A PRAYER FOR TODAY

Selfless Jesus, my heart is overwhelmed by gratitude today. I pray that You would sanctify my imagination as I enter into the story of that night when You washed Your disciples' feet. I sit quietly in the room before You and consider what it would be like to see You wash my feet. I note the emotions and motivations present between us. Jesus, thank You for Your selflessness. Make my heart like Yours. May I always be ready to wash the feet of others through my acts of kindness. May I become like You. May I be selfless, always emptying me of myself to make more room for You. Amen.

Encountering the *Selfless* Jesus:
A PRACTICAL APPLICATION

Remember—these four steps, as explained more fully on pages 23–24 in the introduction, are suggested to help you apply this quality of Christ to your own life.

1. **EXPLORE:** Take time to meditate on this quality of Christ. Use Scriptures in this chapter to get started.

2. **EXPERIENCE:** Turn your meditation into prayer that this quality might impact your life today. Pray the above prayer to begin.

3. **EXPRESS:** During your quiet time, take a moment to journal your thoughts, even if briefly.

4. **EXALT:** Pray, praise or even spontaneously sing your way through today's list of the names of Jesus. It only requires a few minutes.

GLORIFY HIS NAME

Sing to the LORD, praise his *name*; proclaim
his salvation day after day.

PSALM 96:2 NIV, *emphasis added*

Our Majestic Maker Psalm 95:6 TPT

Our Master and Savior 2 Peter 3:18 MSG

Our Mighty One Isaiah 33:21 NLT

Our Only Hope Isaiah 33:2 MSG

Our Passover Lamb 1 Corinthians 5:7 NLT

Our Peace Ephesians 2:14 NKJV

Our Potter Isaiah 64:8 NKJV

Our Reconciling Peace
Ephesians 2:14 TPT

Our Shepherd-Ruler Micah 5:6 MSG

Overseer of Your Souls 1 Peter 2:25 NIV

Paradise of Protection to Me, A
Psalm 61:3 TPT

Patient Power Nahum 1:3 MSG

Peacemaker of the World
Micah 5:4 MSG

Peace Offering, The Leviticus 3:1-5 NKJV

Perfect Hiding Place, A Psalm 9:9 TPT

Perfect Leader, A Hebrews 2:10 NLT

Perfume Poured Out
Song of Solomon 1:3 NIV

Permanent Priest, The Psalm 110:4 MSG

Personal Guide, A Isaiah 42:16 MSG

Personal Rescuer Isaiah 63:9 NLT

Physician Luke 4:23 NKJV

Pioneer and Perfecter of Faith, The
Hebrews 12:2 NIV

Pioneer of Our Salvation
Hebrews 2:10 TPT

Place of Protection, A
Proverbs 18:10 MSG

Place of Safety When I Am in
Distress Psalm 59:16 NLT

Polished Arrow, A Isaiah 49:2 NIV

Portion of My Inheritance, The
Psalm 16:5 NKJV

Power of God, The 1 Corinthians 1:24 NIV

THE
VICTORIOUS
JESUS

Exploring the Wonders of Christ's Triumph

The all-victorious Christ is like a great rock in a weary land, to
whose shelter we may flee in every time of sorrow or trial, find-
ing quiet refuge and peace in him.

J. R. MILLER

LONG-LASTING VICTORY can never be separated from a
long-lasting stand on the foundation of the cross,"[1] wrote Watchman Nee. Nee, a dynamic young Christian leader in China, had
a profound impact on the spread of the Gospel across China during the
first half of the twentieth century. Born in 1903, Nee, at just nineteen
years of age in 1922, initiated multiple church gatherings in Fuzhou,
capital city of China's Fujian province. Many believe this began the
powerful house church movement that would one day have a sweeping
impact across all of China, representing many branches of evangelical
Christianity. Watchman Nee taught much on the victorious Christian
life, and he is a worthy writer to introduce us to the *Victorious Jesus*:

> Outside of Christ, I am only a sinner, but in Christ, I am saved. Out-
> side of Christ, I am empty; in Christ, I am full. Outside of Christ,
> I am weak; in Christ, I am strong. Outside of Christ, I cannot; in

Christ, I am more than able. Outside of Christ, I have been defeated; in Christ, I am already victorious. How meaningful are the words, "in Christ."[2]

A Perpetual Victory Parade

The apostle Paul paints a picture of the believer's victory, uniquely highlighting the two words Watchman Nee referenced repeatedly in his testimony—"in Christ!" Paul wrote:

> In the Messiah, *in Christ,* God leads us from place to place in one perpetual victory parade. Through us, he brings knowledge of Christ. Everywhere we go, people breathe in the exquisite fragrance. Because of Christ, we give off a sweet scent rising to God, which is recognized by those on the way of salvation—an aroma redolent with life.
>
> 2 Corinthians 2:14–16 msg, *emphasis added*

What a glorious parade it is, especially knowing Christ Himself is the parade's Grand Marshal.

Throughout Paul's writings, he would return to this theme of the believer's victory in Christ. To Christians at Rome, the apostle offered these words of encouragement:

> Can anything ever separate us from Christ's love? Does it mean he no longer loves us if we have trouble or calamity, or are persecuted, or hungry, or destitute, or in danger, or threatened with death? . . . No, despite all these things, overwhelming victory is ours through Christ, who loved us.
>
> Romans 8:35, 37 nlt

Two Words of Power

We began this chapter with a reminder that our victory is assured in just two words: "in Christ." But there are two additional words we ought to pay close attention to when reading God's Word. Ray C. Stedman highlights these two words of power, offering this suggestion:

> If you want a wonderful experience, take your New Testament and use a concordance to look up the two little words, *but God*. See how many times human resources have been brought to an utter end; despair has gripped the heart . . . and there is nothing that can be done. Then see how the Spirit of God writes in luminous letters, *but God*, and the whole situation changes into victory.[3]

I recently did exactly that. I quickly found numerous examples in Scripture highlighting key "but God" moments! One was in Peter's sermon on the Day of Pentecost to a curious Jerusalem crowd. The apostle preached:

> "People of Israel, listen! God publicly endorsed Jesus the Nazarene by doing powerful miracles, wonders, and signs through him, as you well know. *But God* knew what would happen. . . . You nailed him to a cross and killed him. *But God* released him from the horrors of death and raised him back to life, for death could not keep him in its grip."
>
> ACTS 2:22–24 NLT, *emphasis added*

Later, when a crippled beggar is healed at the Gate Beautiful (Acts 3), Peter again takes advantage of the moment by preaching to a fascinated crowd of onlookers. He proclaims: "You rejected this holy, righteous one and instead demanded the release of a murderer. You killed the author of life, *but God* raised him from the dead. And we are witnesses of this fact!" (Acts 3:14–15 NLT, emphasis added).

The "But God" Factor

Paul, too, had his "but God" moments. When preaching in Antioch of Pisidia along with his coworker Barnabas, Paul described the immediate aftermath of the crucifixion. He told the crowd: "When [authorities] had done all that the prophecies said about [Jesus], they took him down from the cross and placed him in a tomb. *But God* raised him from the dead!" (Acts 13:29–30 NLT, emphasis added). The "but God" of Christ's resurrection is arguably the greatest "But God" factor in all of Scripture.

Writing to Ephesian believers after the resurrection, Paul would experience yet another "but God" victory moment. The apostle wrote:

> All of us used to live . . . following the passionate desires and inclinations of our sinful nature. By our very nature we were subject to God's anger, just like everyone else. *But God* is so rich in mercy. . . . He gave us life when he raised Christ from the dead.
>
> EPHESIANS 2:3–5 NLT, *emphasis added*

As you walk with the *Victorious Jesus* into this day, and every day, be alert for those special "but God" moments. Fix your eyes continually on Jesus. He is your victory. He is the "author and finisher of our faith" (Hebrews 12:2 NKJV). Heed Bible teacher Alan Redpath's advice: "Any battle for victory, power, and deliverance from ourselves and from sin which is not based constantly upon the gazing and the beholding of the Lord Jesus, with the heart and life lifted up to Him, is doomed to failure."[4]

But thanks be to God, with the *Victorious Jesus* walking beside us, the word *failure* is absent from our vocabulary!

A PRAYER FOR TODAY

I rejoice in Your victory, Jesus! *I celebrate Your victorious life! I worship You, for You stand victorious over death! Jesus, my heart is full of joy today as I meditate on Your victory at the cross. You have triumphed over all death, over all sin, over all evil. I pray that my heart and mind would be truly transformed by Your victory. May I ever walk in Your victory, rest in your victory and rejoice in your victory. I pray I would live in freedom from the fear of death and freedom from the power of sin. May Your victory release new life in me daily, O victorious Savior! Amen.*

Encountering the *Victorious* Jesus:
A PRACTICAL APPLICATION

Remember—these four steps, as explained more fully on pages 23–24 in the introduction, are suggested to help you apply this quality of Christ to your own life.

1. **EXPLORE:** Take time to meditate on this quality of Christ. Use Scriptures in this chapter to get started.

2. **EXPERIENCE:** Turn your meditation into prayer that this quality might impact your life today. Pray the above prayer to begin.

3. **EXPRESS:** During your quiet time, take a moment to journal your thoughts, even if briefly.

4. **EXALT:** Pray, praise or even spontaneously sing your way through today's list of the names of Jesus. It only requires a few minutes.

GLORIFY HIS NAME

Give thanks to the LORD, call on his *name*; make
known among the nations what he has done.

PSALM 105:1 NIV1984, *emphasis added*

Praise-Lofty, The 2 Samuel 22:4 MSG

Preacher of Good News, A
Isaiah 41:27 MSG

Precious Cornerstone 1 Peter 2:6 NIV

Present Everywhere Jeremiah 23:24 MSG

Priest for Eternity, A Psalm 110:4 TPT

Priest Forever, A Hebrews 5:6 NKJV

Priest-Friend 1 John 2:1 MSG

Priest-Mediator 1 Timothy 2:5 MSG

Priest-of-My-Altar Psalm 19:14 MSG

Prince and Savior Acts 5:31 NKJV

Prince of All Princes, The
Daniel 8:25 MSG

Prince of Life, The Acts 3:15 NKJV

Prince of Peace Isaiah 9:6 NLT

Prince of Wholeness Isaiah 9:6 MSG

Propitiation for Our Sins, The
1 John 2:2 NKJV

Provider of Grace Acts 5:31 TPT

Pure God Through and Through
Exodus 15:3 MSG

Rabbi John 1:49 NKJV

Radiant Presence, A Zechariah 2:5 MSG

Rain on Freshly Cut Grass
Psalm 72:6 NLT

Rainmaker, The Zechariah 10:1 MSG

Rallying Banner for the Peoples, A
Isaiah 11:10 MSG

Rallying Banner High, Visible to All
Nations Isaiah 11:12 MSG

Ransom, A Mark 10:45 NKJV

Real Bread, The John 6:32 MSG

Real Life 1 John 5:20 MSG

Real Thing, The Jeremiah 10:10 MSG

Real Vine, The John 15:1 MSG

THE
JOYFUL
JESUS

Exploring the Wonders of Christ's Joy

Joy is the infallible sign of the presence of God!

PIERRE TEILHARD DE CHARDIN

"JOY IS DISTINCTLY A CHRISTIAN WORD and a Christian thing," wrote S. D. Gordon, adding, "Joy has its spring deep down inside. And that spring never runs dry, no matter what happens. Only Jesus gives that joy. He had joy, singing its music within, even under the shadow of the cross."[1] Gordon's insights bring our Month in the Son to a valued view of the *Joyful Jesus*.

A study of the supremacy of Christ without highlighting His joy would be incomplete. Yes, Jesus suffered. Yes, He wept with "strong crying and tears" (Hebrews 5:7 KJV). Yes, He agonized in Gethsemane until His sweat was "like drops of blood falling to the ground" (Luke 22:44 NIV). Yet He never lost His joy. We see that joy especially manifest in His priestly prayer recorded in chapter 17 of John's gospel. On behalf of His disciples, Christ prayed: "But now I am returning to you so Father, I pray that they will experience and enter into my joyous delight in you so that it is fulfilled in them and overflows" (John 17:13 TPT).

Earlier in John's gospel, the apostle recorded these cherished words of Christ: "I love each of you with the same love that the Father loves me.... Let my love nourish your hearts.... My purpose for telling you these things is so that the joy that I experience will fill your hearts with overflowing gladness!" (John 15:9–11 TPT).

The Embodiment of Joy

There is no joy in all the world like the pure joy of knowing Jesus. If Jesus is, indeed, the embodiment of joy, it would seem that the more intimately we know Jesus, the more we will experience His joy. Robert Murray McCheyne, mid-nineteenth-century Scottish Presbyterian preacher whom I quoted in an earlier chapter, had a profound impact on many of his generation, especially regarding the discipline of prayer. That impact stretched well beyond his generation and deeply impacted my early years of ministry in the 1970s. During those same years, I was similarly impacted by the life of an American missionary to the Delaware Indians, David Brainerd, who ministered in the early 1700s. What astonished me about both of these men was that they each died at just 29 years of age. But I noticed something else. Even though both of these leaders suffered greatly at times, McCheyne ultimately dying of typhoid fever and Brainerd of tuberculosis, they were both men of extraordinary joy.

Before his death, Robert Murray McCheyne wrote of this joy:

> The purest joy in the world is joy in Christ Jesus. When the Spirit is poured down, His people get very near and clear views of the Lord Jesus.... They come to a personal cleaving to the Lord. They taste that the Lord is gracious.... Sit under His shadow with great delight.[2]

David Brainerd, who suffered unimaginable challenges when ministering among the native Delaware Indians, somehow maintained the same sense of Christ's joy amid all hardship. In his extensive diary, Brainerd mentioned his pain, using that specific word, just 78 times. He mentioned the words *suffer* or *suffering* only 30 times. However, he used the words *delight*, *pleased*, and *pleasure* 227 times and, rather amazingly, the words *joy* and *enjoy* 350 times. Even as Brainerd battled depression and exceedingly poor health, his diary included such entries as, "This has been a sweet . . . happy day to me." Another entry reads, "It appeared such a happiness to have God for my portion that I had rather be any other creature in this lower creation than not come to the enjoyment of God. . . . Lord, endear Thyself more to me!"[3]

Noteworthy is that when David Brainerd died in 1747, he was in the home of Puritan revivalist Jonathan Edwards. It is said that Brainerd's last words were, "I declare now, I am dying. I would not have spent my life otherwise for the whole world!" Brainerd's joy was still clearly evident in those final earthly moments.

A Flag of Joy

To walk beside the *Joyful Jesus,* savoring and sensing the supremacy of His joy, does not necessarily exempt us from suffering. Sam Storms reminds us, "Joy is not necessarily the absence of suffering, it is the presence of God."[4] Earlier in these pages, we highlighted the wonders of the *Abiding Jesus*. The mere presence of Christ in all our seasons of suffering is, in itself, joy. As we walk with Christ daily, we certainly can appreciate the apostle Peter's words:

> In this you greatly rejoice, though now for a little while, if need be, you have been grieved by various trials, that the genuineness

> of your faith, being much more precious than gold that perishes, though it is tested by fire, may be found to praise, honor, and glory at the revelation of Jesus Christ, whom having not seen you love. Though now you do not see Him, yet believing, you rejoice with joy inexpressible and full of glory, receiving the end of your faith—the salvation of your souls.
>
> 1 PETER 1:6–9 NKJV

Having been to England more than forty times during my years of ministry, I still remember something from one of our very first visits in the early 1970s. My wife and I were listening to a guide as we stood outside Buckingham Palace. We noticed high above the palace the British Royal Standard flag was waving. The guide mentioned that whenever the flag was flying above the palace, it meant the monarch was present. Not long after, upon returning to America, I was in a church that sang a chorus undoubtedly originating from this British tradition: "Joy is the flag flown high from the castle of the heart when the king is in residence there!"[5] Those, indeed, who walk daily with the *Joyful Jesus* will have a flag of joy that is always waving!

A PRAYER FOR TODAY

Jesus, I come to You with great joy today! I want to experience even more of Your true, eternal joy. I invite Your joy to transform my life. May Your joy fill my heart with overflowing gladness. May Your delight be fulfilled in me. I long to sit under Your shadow and bask in Your delight! I want to taste of Your graciousness. May Your joy comfort me. May it bring new healing to my sometimes weary emotions.

May the flag of joy wave unceasingly over my being as a sign of Your presence in my life. Lead me ever deeper into Your joy, dear Jesus, for it is my strength! Amen.

Encountering the *Joyful* Jesus:
A PRACTICAL APPLICATION

Remember—these four steps, as explained more fully on pages 23–24 in the introduction, are suggested to help you apply this quality of Christ to your own life.

1. **EXPLORE:** Take time to meditate on this quality of Christ. Use Scriptures in this chapter to get started.

2. **EXPERIENCE:** Turn your meditation into prayer that this quality might impact your life today. Pray the above prayer to begin.

3. **EXPRESS:** During your quiet time, take a moment to journal your thoughts, even if briefly.

4. **EXALT:** Pray, praise or even spontaneously sing your way through today's list of the names of Jesus. It only requires a few minutes.

GLORIFY HIS NAME

Let the *name* of the LORD be praised, both now and forevermore.

PSALM 113:2 NIV, *emphasis added*

Redeemer, The Isaiah 59:20 NLT

Redeemer of Israel Isaiah 49:7 MSG

Refiner and a Purifier, A
Malachi 3:3 NKJV

Refiner of Silver, A Malachi 3:3 MSG

Refreshing of Israel Luke 2:25 TPT

Refuge for His People, A Joel 3:16 NLT

Refuge for the Oppressed, A
Psalm 9:9 NIV

Refuge from the Storm, A
Isaiah 25:4 NKJV

Refuge in Times of Trouble, A
Nahum 1:7 NIV

Refuge to the Needy Isaiah 25:4 NLT

Renewer of My Strength
Psalm 23:3 NLT

Rescuer, The Jeremiah 50:34 MSG

Resting Place Jeremiah 50:6 NKJV

Restorer Psalm 23:3 NKJV

Restores and Revives My Life
Psalm 23:3 TPT

Resurrection, The John 11:25 NKJV

Resurrection and Life John 11:25 MSG

Revealed in a Human Body
1 Timothy 3:16 NLT

Revealer of Mysteries, The
Daniel 2:29 MSG

Revealer of Secrets Daniel 2:29, 47 NKJV

Revelation Light Luke 2:32 TPT

Rewarder, A Hebrews 11:6 NKJV

Rich in Unfailing Love
Nehemiah 9:17 NLT

Righteous Descendant, A
Jeremiah 33:15 NLT

Righteous Judge, The
2 Timothy 4:8 NKJV

Righteous One, The 1 Peter 3:18 MSG

Rising Sun, The Luke 1:78 NIV

River in Flood Stage, A Isaiah 59:19 MSG

THE
RETURNING
JESUS

Exploring the Wonders of Christ's Return

There beats in the heart of every child of God the glorious hope
of Christ's return.

BILLY GRAHAM

ALAN REDPATH, former pastor of Moody Church, Chicago,
preached in a Christmas message, "The immense step from
the Babe at Bethlehem to the living, reigning triumphant Lord
Jesus, returning to Earth for His own people—that is the glorious truth
proclaimed throughout Scripture."[1] Redpath adds, "As the bells ring out
the joys of Christmas, may we also be alert for the final trumpet that will
announce His return, when we shall always be with Him."[2]

We have thus far looked at numerous aspects of Christ's nature and
character and have felt justified to ascribe to each the descriptive adjective *supreme*. Christ is supreme in His beauty and supreme in His
humility. He is supreme in His righteousness and supreme in His compassion. His supremacy touches all of His being, all of His qualities and
everything that might be said of any characteristic to describe Him. He
will be equally and overwhelmingly supreme in His return to earth to
rule and reign for all eternity. So we set aside these moments to bathe
our Month in the Son thoughts with a view of the *Returning Jesus*!

A Cleavage in the Sky

One of the great promises of Christ to His disciples is recorded by John in chapter 14 of his gospel. We recall these familiar words:

> "Let not your heart be troubled; you believe in God, believe also in Me. In My Father's house are many mansions; if it were not so, I would have told you. I go to prepare a place for you. And if I go and prepare a place for you, I will come again and receive you to Myself; that where I am, there you may be also."
>
> JOHN 14:1–3 NKJV

The return of Christ was clearly one of the most cherished doctrines of first-century believers. Paul had described it vividly to the Thessalonian believers:

> We tell you this directly from the Lord: We who are still living when the Lord returns will not meet him ahead of those who have died. For the Lord himself will come down from heaven with a commanding shout, with the voice of the archangel, and with the trumpet call of God. First, the believers who have died will rise from their graves. Then, together with them, we who are still alive and remain on the earth will be caught up in the clouds to meet the Lord in the air. Then we will be with the Lord forever. So encourage each other with these words.
>
> 1 THESSALONIANS 4:15–18 NLT

Alexander MacLaren, reflecting on these words, wrote: "The apostolic church thought more about the Second Coming of Jesus Christ than about death and heaven. The early Christians were looking, not for a cleft in the ground called a grave, but for a cleavage in the sky called Glory."[3]

If You Finish It, He Will Come

A question that understandably arises often is, why has the return of our Lord taken so long? First-century Christians clearly believed Christ's return was imminent. Many evangelical Christians still believe that to be true. He could return at any moment. The apostle Peter perhaps provides the best response to this age-old question. He wrote first-century believers, saying:

> But you must not forget this one thing, dear friends: A day is like a thousand years to the Lord, and a thousand years is like a day. The Lord isn't really being slow about his promise, as some people think. No, he is being patient for your sake. He does not want anyone to be destroyed, but wants everyone to repent.
>
> 2 Peter 3:8–9 NLT

What an extraordinary picture of the supreme patience of God! But God's patience is not only for unbelievers, allowing them time to repent, but it is also for believers, to take the Gospel to the very ends of the earth.

Recall with me Christ's Mount of Olives discourse about His return at the end of the age. The disciples asked an interesting two-part question: "Tell us, when will these things be? And what will be the sign of Your coming, and of the end of the age?" (Matthew 24:3 NKJV). Paying attention to the nuance of these two questions is important. First, they ask a question in the plural tense: "When will these things be?" Christ likewise answers in the plural. He explains that many "things" would happen, like "wars and rumors of wars," "nations rising against nations" and "famines, pestilences, and earthquakes in various places." But He made it clear "the end is not yet."

After describing these "things" that had to happen, Christ answers the disciples' second question: "What will be the sign of Your coming?"

Note, in this question the word "sign" is in the singular. To this question, Christ speaks of only one specific indicator: "And this gospel of the kingdom will be preached in all the world as a witness to all the nations, and then the end will come" (Matthew 24:14 NKJV).

If one ties these words of Christ in Matthew 24 directly to those of the apostle Peter in his second letter explaining the delay of Christ's return (2 Peter 3:8–9, 14), it seems the obedience of Christ's followers to complete the Great Commission is directly related to the return of our Lord. To rephrase the popular movie *Field of Dreams'* most memorable line regarding building a baseball field in rural Iowa for the ghosts of baseball's past to return, *"If you build it, they will come,"*[4] we might well conclude regarding Christ's ultimate return and the commission He gave His disciples, *"If you finish it, He will come!"* Could it be we are the generation of Christ's disciples called to be the finishers?

The return of Christ, indeed, might well be as imminent as the saints of Christ are obedient!

A PRAYER FOR TODAY

Lord Jesus Christ, I long for the day of Your return! My heart aches with anticipation for the restoration of all things under Your eternal reign. With great desire I look forward to the day when You will be enthroned over all heaven and earth. Jesus, fill me increasingly with a heightened awareness of Your imminent return. May my heart stand on tiptoe in awesome anticipation that it could be at any moment! May my life reflect the utter assurance that You are coming soon to make all things new. Oh, what a glorious and joyful day that will be! Amen.

Encountering the *Returning* Jesus:
A PRACTICAL APPLICATION

Remember—these four steps, as explained more fully on pages 23–24 in the introduction, are suggested to help you apply this quality of Christ to your own life.

1. **EXPLORE:** Take time to meditate on this quality of Christ. Use Scriptures in this chapter to get started.

2. **EXPERIENCE:** Turn your meditation into prayer that this quality might impact your life today. Pray the above prayer to begin.

3. **EXPRESS:** During your quiet time, take a moment to journal your thoughts, even if briefly.

4. **EXALT:** Pray, praise or even spontaneously sing your way through today's list of the names of Jesus. It only requires a few minutes.

GLORIFY HIS NAME

From the rising of the sun to the place where it
sets, the *name* of the LORD is to be praised.

PSALM 113:3 NIV, *emphasis added*

Road, Also the Truth, Also the Life,
The John 14:6 MSG

Rock-Firm and Faithful Psalm 73:26 MSG

Rock in Whom I Take Refuge, The
Psalm 94:22 NIV

Rock of Israel, The Isaiah 30:29 NLT

Rock of My Salvation, The
2 Samuel 22:47 NKJV

Rock of Offense, A
1 Peter 2:8; Isaiah 8:14 NKJV

Rock-of-Refuge Isaiah 17:10 MSG

Rock of Your Stronghold, The
Isaiah 17:10 NKJV

Rock-Solid God Habakkuk 1:12 MSG

Rock That Is Higher Than I, The
Psalm 61:2 NKJV

Rock Where No Enemy Can Reach
Me, A Psalm 62:7 NLT

Rock Who Saved Us, The
Psalm 95:1 MSG

Rock, Your Fortress, The
Isaiah 17:10 NIV

Rod from the Stem of Jesse, A
Isaiah 11:1 NKJV

Rod of Your Strength, The
Psalm 110:2 NKJV

Root Out of Dry Ground, A
Isaiah 53:2 NKJV

Rose of Sharon, The
Song of Solomon 2:1 NKJV

Royal Son, The Psalm 72:1 NIV

Ruler Micah 5:2 NLT

Ruler of All Earthly Kings
Revelation 1:5 MSG

Ruler of All the Kings of the World,
The Revelation 1:5 NLT

Ruler of God's Creation
Revelation 3:14 TPT

Ruler Passionate for Justice, A
Isaiah 16:5 MSG

Ruler Quick to Set Things Right, A
Isaiah 16:5 MSG

Ruler Who Knows How to Rule
Justly, A Jeremiah 23:5 MSG

Ruler You Can Depend Upon, A
Isaiah 16:5 MSG

Sachet of Sweet Myrrh, A
Song of Solomon 1:13 MSG

Sacred Manna, The Revelation 2:17 MSG

Sacrifice for Sin, The Romans 3:25 NLT

THE
GLORIOUS
JESUS

Exploring the Wonders of Christ's Glory

Jesus is not merely the vessel through whom the glory of God is communicated; he himself is the very content of that glory within the vessel.

DAVID BRYANT

A. B. SIMPSON, founder of The Christian and Missionary Alliance in 1887, had a profound impact through both his preaching and writing. On one occasion, as Simpson preached to a hall full of passionate believers, he described one of the most foundational realities of the Christian life. In so doing, he brings us to our view of the *Glorious Jesus*. Simpson declared:

> If I could stand on this platform and say, "I have received from heaven a secret of wealth and success which God will give freely, through my hand, to everybody who will take it," I am sure you would need a larger hall for the people who would come. But, dear friends, I show you in His Word a truth which is more precious, a great secret which is now disclosed to the saints. . . . That simple secret is this: "Christ in you, the hope of glory." I feel I have only begun to learn how well it works.[1]

The apostle Paul, in writing to the Colossian believers, spoke of "the mystery which has been hidden from ages and from generations, but now has been revealed to His saints" (Colossians 1:26 NKJV). Paul then explained that it was now God's will "to make known what are the riches of the glory of this mystery" (verse 27 NKJV). The apostle then reveals this seven-word foundational summary that could easily be described as the very essence of the Gospel of Christ: "Christ in you, the hope of glory" (verse 27 NKJV).

The Grand Summation of Glory

In recent chapters, we spoke of the *Victorious Jesus*, the *Joyful Jesus*, and the *Returning Jesus*. All these qualities are related to the supremacy of Christ's glory. Jesus is, quite simply, supremely glorious. In writing to the Corinthian believers, Paul refers to Christ as our "glorious Lord" (1 Corinthians 2:8 NLT) or "the Lord of glory" (1 Corinthians 2:8 NIV). The word *glory* expresses excellence of the highest level. Christ is more than mere excellence—He is the Lord of excellence. He is excellence in the supreme.

The Greek word for *excellence* is *doxa* (from which we get our word *doxology*), which means "brightness" or "radiance." *Brightness* means "brilliancy, splendor and illumination." It suggests an explosive, blinding brightness that illuminates the Lord in all His majestic splendor and glory.[2] Quite simply, *Christ is the grand summation of glory!* Paul suggests this when he wrote to the Corinthian believers: "For it is the God who commanded light to shine out of darkness, who has shone in our hearts to *give* the light of the knowledge of the glory of God in the face of Jesus Christ" (2 Corinthians 4:6, NKJV).

Many of the psalmist's songs also highlight our glorious Lord. A psalm of David declares: "Open the ancient gates, so that the glorious king may come in. Who is this glorious king? He is our LORD, a strong and mighty warrior" (Psalm 24:7–8 CEV). On another occasion, the psalmist sang, "I praise you, LORD God, with all my heart. You are glorious and majestic, dressed in royal robes and surrounded by light" (Psalm 104:1–2 CEV).

To capture something of this same wonder of God's glory, the believer must spend much time intimately with God's Son. We return again to the opening words of Hebrews: "The Son radiates God's own glory and expresses the very character of God, and he sustains everything by the mighty power of his command" (Hebrews 1:3 NLT).

A Landscape of Glory

One day all who know and follow Christ as Savior will experience God's glory and the wonder of His glorious Son, Jesus, in a truly "otherworldly" way. We will shed our human bodies to receive heavenly bodies suited for eternity. Paul explained this in his letter to the Philippian believers: "For our citizenship is in heaven, from which we also eagerly wait for the Savior, the Lord Jesus Christ, who will transform our lowly body that it may be conformed to His glorious body, according to the working by which He is able even to subdue all things to Himself" (Philippians 3:20–21 NKJV). What an awesome day it will be when our bodies are transformed and conformed to be like Christ's glorious body!

But for now, we can experience Christ's glory by basking often and long in His awesome presence. And we can labor together to see Christ's glory flood the earth through the spreading of His glorious Gospel. Imagine if we could see something happen globally like described in Ezekiel's vision when he wrote, "Suddenly, the glory of the God of Israel appeared from the east. The sound of his coming was like the roar of rushing waters, and the whole landscape shown with his glory" (Ezekiel

43:2 NLT). Imagine the landscape of our nation and world filled with God's glory! Could it be that our generation will live to see Habakkuk's prophecy literally fulfilled, "For as the waters fill the sea, the earth will be filled with an awareness of the glory of the LORD" (Habakkuk 2:14 NLT)?

May we join King David and his worship leader Asaph in a stanza from David's song composed when the king initiated 24/7 worship in the tent he pitched in Jerusalem to contain the Ark of God:

> Let the whole earth sing to the LORD! Each day proclaim the good news that he saves. Publish his glorious deeds among the nations. Tell everyone about the amazing things he does. . . . O nations of the world, recognize the LORD, recognize that the LORD is glorious and strong.
>
> 1 CHRONICLES 16:23–24, 28 NLT

A PRAYER FOR TODAY

Glorious Jesus, majestic and mighty and worthy of praise, I worship You today! I set my heart on Your glory, and I am overwhelmed by who You are, Lord. Everything about You, every finite detail, makes You all the more glorious. I pray that You would be glorified in me throughout all my days, Jesus. I pray that every day I would discover Your glory in new ways so that I might reflect the radiance of Your presence wherever I go. In everything I say and think, may I bring glory to You, dear Savior. Your glory is all I truly long for! Be glorified in my life, Jesus! Amen.

Encountering the *Glorious* Jesus:
A PRACTICAL APPLICATION

Remember—these four steps, as explained more fully on pages 23–24 in the introduction, are suggested to help you apply this quality of Christ to your own life.

1. **EXPLORE:** Take time to meditate on this quality of Christ. Use Scriptures in this chapter to get started.

2. **EXPERIENCE:** Turn your meditation into prayer that this quality might impact your life today. Pray the above prayer to begin.

3. **EXPRESS:** During your quiet time, take a moment to journal your thoughts, even if briefly.

4. **EXALT:** Pray, praise or even spontaneously sing your way through today's list of the names of Jesus. It only requires a few minutes.

GLORIFY HIS NAME

Not to us, O LORD, not to us but to your *name* be the
glory, because of your love and faithfulness.

PSALM 115:1 NIV1984, *emphasis added*

Sacrifice of Atonement, A
Romans 3:25 NIV

Safe-Harbor-God Psalm 62:7 MSG

Safe Hiding Place, A Joel 3:16 MSG

Safe-House for the Battered, A
Psalm 9:9 MSG

Safe Leader Psalm 31:5 MSG

Safe Place for Me, A Psalm 59:16 MSG

Safe Place for Those on the Run, A
Isaiah 16:3 MSG

Safe Place to Be, A Psalm 62:8 MSG

Safe Refuge Psalm 61:3 NLT

Salvation of Israel, The
Jeremiah 3:22 MSG

Salvation Pioneer, The
Hebrews 2:10 MSG

Sanctuary, A Isaiah 8:14 NKJV

Sanctuary during Bad Times, A
Psalm 9:9 MSG

Savior and Champion Acts 5:31 TPT

Savior and Rescuer, A Daniel 6:27 MSG

Savior God Isaiah 45:15 MSG

Savior of the World 1 John 4:14 NLT

Savior Who Will Keep Them Safe,
A Isaiah 19:19 MSG

Secret Hiding Place Psalm 32:7 TPT

Shade from the Heat, A
Isaiah 25:4 NKJV

Shadow of a Great Rock in a
Weary Land, The Isaiah 32:2 NKJV

Sheep Being Sheared, A
Isaiah 53:7 MSG

Sheer Beauty Psalm 100:5 MSG

Sheer Grace and Mercy Jonah 4:2 MSG

Sheer Wonder Judges 13:18 MSG

Shelter for His People, A Joel 3:16 NKJV

Shelter from High Winds, A
Isaiah 32:2 MSG

Shelter from the Storm Isaiah 25:4 MSG

THE
STEADFAST
JESUS

Exploring the Wonders
of Christ's Steadfastness

*Lord, give me firmness without hardness, steadfastness without
dogmatism, love without weakness.*

JIM ELLIOT

FROM THE OUTSET of Christ's earthly ministry, one quality
that marked His life continually was His steadfast determination
to fulfill the will of His Father. Indeed, when it was time for Him
to face the cross, Luke records: "Now it came to pass, when the time had
come for Him to be received up, that He steadfastly set His face to go
to Jerusalem" (Luke 9:51 NKJV). The New Living Translation translates
this verse: "As the time drew near for him to ascend to heaven, Jesus
resolutely set out for Jerusalem."

The prophet Isaiah had foretold this moment when he wrote of the
Messiah: "I gave My back to those who struck Me. . . . I did not hide
My face from shame and spitting. For the Lord GOD will help Me. . . .
Therefore I have set My face like a flint, and I know that I will not be
ashamed" (Isaiah 50:6–7 NKJV).

Christ's ministry was constantly marked with His steadfast spirit. *Steadfast* is defined as: "firm, fixed, settled, or established; unchanging, unwavering, constant and consistent." Every word describes Jesus. Our *Month in the Son* brings us to a compelling view of the *Steadfast Jesus!*

Lord of the Must

Years ago, while I was reading the gospel of John, I paused to meditate on the intensity of a single phrase from the lips of Jesus: "I must work the works of him that sent me" (John 9:4 KJV). In those early days of my ministry, most, if not all, of my Bible reading and teaching focused on the King James Version of Scripture. The word *must* seized my attention. Jesus did not say, "I've thought about doing this," or, "It is My intention to do this." No, Jesus said emphatically, "I *must!*" Here we see something of Christ's steadfast determination manifesting itself. He is the Lord of the *must!* I quickly discovered Christ only used the word *must* eight times. I will highlight each of these instances briefly for you.

First was the *must* of *duty.* Christ as a twelve-year-old had been taken to Jerusalem by His family for a ceremony referred to as the Bar Mitzvah. Jesus somehow was separated from the family, and three days later, Mary and Joseph found Him still in the Temple. When His mother anxiously told Jesus they had been looking for Him, He responded, "Did you not know that I must be about My Father's business?" (Luke 2:48–49 NKJV). Of course, the "Father's business" just happened to be the redemption of humankind.

Second was the *must* of *suffering.* Gospel writer Mark records: "And He [Christ] began to teach them that the Son of Man must suffer many things, and be rejected" (Mark 8:31 KJV). Here Christ is referring to

Himself in the third person, stating His ultimate suffering, rejection and even death on the cross was a must!

Third was the *must* of *mission*. Luke, in describing Christ's ministry near Capernaum, records:

> Now when it was day, [Jesus] departed and went into a deserted place. And the crowd sought Him and came to Him, and tried to keep Him from leaving them; but He said to them, "I must preach the kingdom of God to the other cities also, because for this purpose I have been sent."
>
> Luke 4:42–43 nkjv

Here Christ confirms His commitment to His ultimate mission—to establish the Kingdom of God everywhere.

Fourth was the *must* of *persistence*. As Jesus drew ever closer to the cross, He still ministered from village to village. The Pharisees approached Christ one day with a stern warning: "Get out and depart from here, for Herod wants to kill You" (Luke 13:31 nkjv). Jesus immediately replied, "Go, tell that fox . . . I must journey today, tomorrow, and the day following; for it cannot be that a prophet should perish outside of Jerusalem" (Luke 13:32–33 nkjv). This was Christ's way of saying, "I must keep persevering until My appointed time with the cross arrives!"

Fifth was the *must* of *relationship*. One day the Lord passed through Jericho, where large crowds had gathered. Everyone was stretching and straining for a view of Jesus. One of those, a tax collector named Zacchaeus, had climbed a tree to catch a better glimpse. Luke writes: "And when Jesus came to the place, He looked up and saw him, and said to him, 'Zacchaeus, make haste and come down, for today I must stay at your house'" (Luke 19:5 nkjv). This was Christ's commitment to relationships. He went to where people lived.

Sixth was the *must* of *sacrifice*. Christ knew the cross was His destiny. Speaking in the third person, He said: "As Moses lifted up the serpent in the wilderness, even so must the Son of Man be lifted up" (John 3:14 NKJV). Christ's reference to being "lifted up" was clearly a reference to the cross. To Christ, the cross was a must!

Seventh was the *must* of *opportunity*. When Christ healed a blind man, His disciples asked, "Rabbi, who sinned, this man or his parents, that he was born blind?" (John 9:2 NKJV). Jesus responded: "Neither . . . but that the works of God should be revealed in him." Christ then added, "I must work the works of Him who sent Me while it is day; the night is coming when no one can work" (John 9:3–4 NKJV). This was the *must* of the *now*!

Eighth was the *must* of *completion*. In John 10, Christ described His final divine must: "And other sheep I have which are not of this fold; them also I must bring, and they will hear My voice; and there will be one flock and one shepherd" (John 10:16 NKJV). Of course, all followers of Christ have been invited to participate in helping carry out Christ's final "must" assignment. His *must* is now our *must*!

Christ's "other sheep" mandate is our mandate. We must pray. We must weep. We must give. We must go. We must join the *Steadfast Jesus* in finishing the task. We are all called to join Christ's last days' "company of finishers"!

A PRAYER FOR TODAY

Jesus, I thank You today for Your steadfastness. I am humbled as I focus my attention on all Your steadfast love has meant for me personally. Lord, I want to be challenged and changed by Your steadfast example. I want to walk in Your ways with a steadfast determination and submit to suffering as You did. I want to embrace Your mission with a steadfast abandonment. May I declare each day as You declared as a child—"I must be about My Father's business." May I be ready to steadfastly embrace every opportunity to honor Your name in all I do. Amen.

Encountering the *Steadfast* Jesus:
A PRACTICAL APPLICATION

Remember—these four steps, as explained more fully on pages 23–24 in the introduction, are suggested to help you apply this quality of Christ to your own life.

1. **EXPLORE:** Take time to meditate on this quality of Christ. Use Scriptures in this chapter to get started.

2. **EXPERIENCE:** Turn your meditation into prayer that this quality might impact your life today. Pray the above prayer to begin.

3. **EXPRESS:** During your quiet time, take a moment to journal your thoughts, even if briefly.

4. **EXALT:** Pray, praise or even spontaneously sing your way through today's list of the names of Jesus. It only requires a few minutes.

GLORIFY HIS NAME

Our help is in the *name* of the LORD, the
Maker of heaven and earth.

PSALM 124:8 NIV, *emphasis added*

Shelter in the Time of Trouble, A
Psalm 9:9 TPT

**Shepherd and Overseer of Your
Souls, The** 1 Peter 2:25 NIV

Shepherd-King, The 1 Peter 5:4 TPT

Shepherd of Israel Psalm 80:1 NKJV

Shepherd of Your Souls, The
1 Peter 2:25 MSG

Shield and Helper
Deuteronomy 33:29 NIV

Shield Who Defends You, The
Deuteronomy 33:29 MSG

Singular and Sovereign Job 23:13 MSG

Sinless, Spotless Lamb of God, The
1 Peter 1:19 NLT

Solid Rock under My Feet
Psalm 62:2, 6 MSG

Son of God, The John 1:34 NKJV

Son of Mary, The Mark 6:3 NKJV

Son of the Father, The 2 John 3 NKJV

Son of the Highest, The Luke 1:32 NKJV

Source of Eternal Salvation, The
Hebrews 5:9 NLT

Source of Every Human Alive, The
1 Corinthians 11:3 TPT

Source of Hope, The Romans 15:13 NLT

Source of Life, The 1 Peter 2:4 MSG

Source of Love and Peace, The
2 Corinthians 13:11 TPT

Sovereign Lord Psalm 68:20 NIV

Spirit of Justice, A Isaiah 28:6 NKJV

**Spirit That Brings Wisdom and
Understanding, The** Isaiah 11:2 MSG

Spiritual Rock, The 1 Corinthians 10:4 NLT

Splendor Light, The Luke 1:78 TPT

**Spreading Fragrance of Scented
Oils, The** Song of Solomon 1:3 NLT

Spring of Living Water, The
Jeremiah 17:13 NIV

Spring Thunderstorm Maker
Zechariah 10:1 MSG

Star Rising from Jacob, A
Numbers 24:17 NLT

THE

PREEMINENT

JESUS

Exploring the Wonders
of Christ's Preeminence

His Son is God the Word, and Wisdom, and Truth, and
Righteousness—and everything else that the sacred Scriptures
call him when speaking of God.

ORIGEN (AD 248)

"W HEN THE DRAMA OF HISTORY is over," wrote
German theologian Helmut Thielicke, "Jesus Christ will
stand alone on the stage. All the great figures of history . . .
will realize that they have been actors in a drama produced by another."[1]

Our journey of enjoying a Month in the Son brings us to a place
of exploring and experiencing Christ's awesome preeminence. He is
the *Preeminent Jesus*. *Preeminent* has a variety of meanings, including: "above all others; excelling others; excellent; surpassing all others;
supreme; superb; marvelous." *Preeminent* is related to *predominant*,
meaning "having ascendency," "dominating all others." Admittedly,
the words *supreme* and *preeminent* seem to define each other. Yet, I
feel very comfortable referring to Christ as supremely preeminent and
preeminently supreme.

A Road to Christ

The apostle Paul would combine the two words *supreme* and *preeminent* when he described Christ to Colossian believers: "He is also the head [the life-source and leader] of the body, the church; and He is the beginning, the firstborn from the dead, so that He Himself will occupy the first place [He will stand supreme and be preeminent] in everything" (Colossians 1:18 AMP).

Paul wrote this to Christians in Philippi:

> So God lifted him up to the highest place. God gave him the name that is above every name. When the name of Jesus is spoken, everyone will kneel down to worship him. Everyone in heaven and on earth and under the earth will kneel down to worship him. Everyone's mouth will say that Jesus Christ is Lord. And God the Father will receive the glory.
>
> PHILIPPIANS 2:9–11 NIRV

A phrase that especially stands out in Paul's message to the Philippian believers are the ten words: "God gave him the name that is above every name!" No personality in the history of humankind has had the impact of the carpenter's son from Nazareth named Jesus. His preeminence is uncontested and His supremacy undisputed.

John Knox, founder of the Presbyterian Church of Scotland and key leader of the Protestant Reformation in Scotland in the mid-1500s, had such great spiritual influence that Mary, Queen of Scots, once said: "I fear the prayers of John Knox more than all the assembled armies of Europe."[2]

The preeminence of Christ was central to the preaching and writings of Knox. Of his preaching, it was said: "Christ is in every noun, in every adverb, in every adjective, in every participle. . . ."[3]

The same was true of Charles Spurgeon. He wrote: "Whatever subject I preach, I do not stop until I reach the Savior, the Lord Jesus, for in Him are all things." To fellow preachers, Spurgeon offered this challenge: "From every text of Scripture there is a road to Christ. And my dear brother, your business is, when you get to a text, to say, now, what is the road to Christ? I have never found a text that did not have a road to Christ in it."[4]

Supreme Soul Seeker

Throughout our Month in the Son together, I have included hundreds of names and phrases that describe our awesome Lord. Certainly, one of the most significant of these is the simple phrase—*the Lord Jesus Christ!* The *Preeminent Jesus* is seen in each word of this name.

First, we must not skip too quickly over the definite article *the*, which begins His name. A key definition of *the* reads: "that (one) designated or identified" and "that (one) considered outstanding." There clearly is only one Person in the entire universe who is worthy of the title—*the* Lord Jesus Christ.

Next is the name *Lord*, meaning, "one having great power and authority; ruler; master." We have shared multiple examples of Scripture in the previous pages to describe Christ as "Lord of All"! Luke writes in his apostolic account of the growing early Church, "This is the same message that God gave to the people of Israel, when he sent Jesus Christ, the Lord of all, to offer peace to them" (Acts 10:36 CEV).

Then comes the beautiful expression we have spoken of so often in these pages—*Jesus*! This name literally means "Jehovah saves!"[5] When Christ came in the flesh to live among humankind, He clearly stated His mission when He told Zacchaeus, a chief tax collector: "For the Son of Man has come to seek and to save that which was lost" (Luke 19:10 NKJV). Christ is the supreme soul seeker!

Finally, Jesus is called the Christ. This title comes from the Greek word translated "anointed one." In Hebrew, the equivalent to the name *Christ* is *Messiah*. The apostle Peter, while preaching to a Jerusalem crowd on the Day of Pentecost, declared, "Can't you see it? God has resurrected Jesus, and we all have seen him! Then God exalted him to his right hand upon the throne of highest honor" (Acts 2:32–33 TPT). Peter quickly adds, "Now everyone in Israel can know for certain that Jesus, whom you crucified, is the one God has made both Lord and the Messiah" (Acts 2:36 TPT).

Paul provides some final, vital words of Christ's Messianic preeminence. Describing his prayers for Ephesian believers, he wrote:

> I also pray that you will understand the incredible greatness of God's power . . . the same mighty power that raised Christ from the dead and seated him in the place of honor at God's right hand in the heavenly realms. Now he is far above any ruler or authority or power or leader or anything else—not only in this world but also in the world to come.
>
> EPHESIANS 1:19–21 NLT

Have you seen Jesus today in His supreme preeminence? Puritan revivalist Jonathan Edwards provides this worthy summary to our view of the *Preeminent Jesus*: "Jesus Christ has true excellency, and so great an excellency, that when you come to truly see Him, you look no further, but your mind rests there."[6]

A PRAYER FOR TODAY

Preeminent Jesus, You reign over all! You are above all things, within all things, first in all things. Jesus, my Lord and Savior, I invite You today and every day to be preeminent in my life. May I wake each morning conscious of Your supreme preeminence. Just as the great preachers followed the texts of Scripture discovering every road that leads to You, I pray I would find new roads to Your preeminent presence every moment of my life. Be above all things in my heart. Reign above all things in my soul. Be first, O Lord, in all I think and do! I worship You alone! Amen.

Encountering the *Preeminent* Jesus:
A PRACTICAL APPLICATION

Remember—these four steps, as explained more fully on pages 23–24 in the introduction, are suggested to help you apply this quality of Christ to your own life.

1. **EXPLORE:** Take time to meditate on this quality of Christ. Use Scriptures in this chapter to get started.

2. **EXPERIENCE:** Turn your meditation into prayer that this quality might impact your life today. Pray the above prayer to begin.

3. **EXPRESS:** During your quiet time, take a moment to journal your thoughts, even if briefly.

4. **EXALT:** Pray, praise or even spontaneously sing your way through today's list of the names of Jesus. It only requires a few minutes.

GLORIFY HIS NAME

Your *name*, O Lord, endures forever, your
renown, O Lord, through all generations.

Psalm 135:13 niv1984, *emphasis added*

Stone in Zion, A 1 Peter 2:6 msg

Stone of Israel, The Genesis 49:24 nkjv

Stone of Stumbling, A 1 Peter 2:8 nkjv

Stone the Builders Rejected, The
1 Peter 2:7 niv

Stone the Workmen Threw Out,
The 1 Peter 2:7 msg

Stone to Be Proud Of, A 1 Peter 2:7 msg

Streams of Water in the Desert
Isaiah 32:2 niv

Strength to the Needy, A
Isaiah 25:4 nkjv

Strength to the Poor, A Isaiah 25:4 nkjv

Strong God Isaiah 9:6 msg

Stronghold, A Nahum 1:7 nkjv

Stronghold in Times of Trouble, A
Psalm 9:9 niv

Stronghold of My Life, The
Psalm 27:1 niv

Stronghold of Salvation, A
Psalm 31:3 tpt

Strong King Psalm 99:4 msg

Strong Lord, A Psalm 89:8 kjv

Strong Tower, A Psalm 61:3 nkjv

Strong Warrior, A Zephaniah 3:17 msg

Sun and Our Shield Psalm 84:11 nlt

Sun and Shield, A Psalm 84:11 nkjv

Sun of Righteousness, The
Malachi 4:2 nkjv

Sure Foundation, A Isaiah 28:16 nkjv

Surety, A Hebrews 7:22 nkjv

Sustaining All Things by His
Powerful Word Hebrews 1:3 niv

Sword of Your Majesty, The
Deuteronomy 33:29 nkjv

Sword Who Brings Triumph, The
Deuteronomy 33:29 msg

Teacher Matthew 23:8 nkjv

Teacher and Lord John 13:13 nlt

THE
ETERNAL
JESUS

Exploring the Wonders
of Christ's Changelessness

Jesus Christ, by coming into this world, has changed the sunsets of time into the sunrises of eternity.

CLEMENT OF ALEXANDRA (AD 150–215)

GEORGE MÜLLER WAS A GIANT of the Christian faith who believed God for great things in caring for orphans in nineteenth-century England. By his death at age 92 in 1898, Müller had cared for more than ten thousand orphans and started 117 schools providing Christian education to some 120,000 children. He was known for his extraordinary faith. He never organized a fund-raising campaign for his ministry. He simply prayed for the resources necessary to care for his many orphans. Müller labored with one eye on his work and the other on eternity. He trusted that the same miracle-working Christ of the New Testament was still the miracle-working Christ among his many orphans. Müller introduces us to the *Eternal Jesus*, our changeless, timeless, limitless Lord. In his voluminous journals, which contained more than 55,000 handwritten answers to prayer, Müller once wrote:

> While all things change here below, the precious Jesus, our Friend,
> is "the same yesterday, and today, and forever." What He was
> millions of years ago, He is now. What He was when He walked
> through Judaea, Samaria, and Galilee, He is now—His heart full of
> tenderness, of pity, of compassion. Oh, how patient, how loving,
> how gracious! Oh, what a lovely Being Jesus is![1]

The End of the Old

To walk daily with the *Eternal Jesus* is not only to recognize Christ's
changelessness, but to cultivate an ever-expanding understanding
and awareness of eternity. Eternity-focused believers are vessels in the
hands of the Lord to change the destiny of men and nations. C. S. Lewis
wisely observed: "If you read history you will find that the Christians
who did most for the present world were precisely those who thought
most of the next."[2] Dietrich Bonhoeffer mused:

> The world dreams of progress, power and of the future. Disciples
> meditate on the End. . . . The Church of Christ bears witness to
> the end of all things. It lives from the end, it thinks from the end.
> . . . Christ is the new, Christ is the end of the old. . . . Therefore, the
> Scriptures need to be read and proclaimed wholly from the view-
> point of the end.[3]

The apostle John wrote of the *Eternal Jesus*: "This one who is life
itself was revealed to us, and we have seen him. And now we testify and
proclaim to you that he is the one who is eternal life" (1 John 1:2 NLT).
Later in that same letter, the apostle added, "And we know that the Son
of God has come, and he has given us understanding so that we can
know the true God. . . . He is the only true God, and he is eternal life"
(1 John 5:20 NLT). The focus of Scripture is always on eternity.

The Future Starts Now

As we journey with the *Eternal Jesus* day by day, we have the extraordinary joy of knowing the journey will continue into forever—a future of endless heavenly delight. The journey here on earth may have its momentary challenges. Believers are not exempt from temptations, tests and trials. Author Max Lucado is right: "God never said that the journey would be easy, but He did say that the arrival would be worthwhile."[4] That gives us hope. And hope gives us courage. In the *end* we will prevail. In the *now* we must persevere. Believers have everything to live for and an eternity to enjoy it!

The apostle Peter spoke of this hope when he wrote:

> What a God we have! And how fortunate we are to have him, this Father of our Master Jesus! Because Jesus was raised from the dead, we've been given a brand-new life and have everything to live for, including a future in heaven—and the future starts now!
>
> 1 Peter 1:3–4 msg

Eternity ought to be on the mind of every believer, every day. Eternity is forever, and forever is never over! In his early life, C. S. Lewis, a brilliant thinker, was an atheist. His life was later transformed through encountering Christ as Savior. God then used the great mind of C. S. Lewis greatly to influence many to understand the reality of the *Eternal Jesus*! Lewis spoke often of eternity. Once he wrote,

> Christianity asserts that every individual human being is going to live forever, and this must be either true or false. Now there are a good many things which would not be worth bothering about if I were going to live only seventy years, but which I had better bother about very seriously if I am going to live forever.[5]

The Brink of Eternity

Have you thought much lately about eternity? A memorable line in the diary of David Brainerd reads: "I love to live on the brink of eternity."[6] So how are we preparing for our eternal destiny? I have spoken in hundreds of churches and conferences throughout the world over more than five decades of ministry, often circling the globe five or six times in a single year. I have lost count of the times I have begun a message with two simple questions. First: "How many here are on your way to heaven?" Because most in the crowd are believers, hands go up everywhere. Second, I ask: "How many want to take a lot of people with you?" Hands, likewise, shoot up everywhere across the crowd. I know that is the secret desire of every believer.

I then remind listeners that no believer should go to heaven without a harvest. We need to be eternity-conscious and harvest-conscious! Jesus spoke of laying up "treasures in heaven, where neither moth nor rust destroys and where thieves do not break in and steal" (Matthew 6:20 NKJV). This is having one eye on the *now* and the other on the *future*. I know of no greater treasure to take to heaven than that of redeemed souls who will become eternal worshipers for Jesus.

A PRAYER FOR TODAY

Eternal Jesus, I come before You today celebrating Your timeless, changeless, eternal presence. You are ever and always—yesterday, today and forever! And because You are eternal, and living in me, I, too, am eternal and dwelling in You. I am overwhelmed by these thoughts, but I know they are true. I can only imagine the wonder of spending eternity with You. It is far beyond my comprehension. O Jesus, flood my mind and heart with the glorious hope of eternity in Your presence. May my perspective on life be defined by the truth of eternity. May my motivations be marked by the reality of eternity. I want to live my life in view of eternity. I praise You, Jesus, for You are eternal! Amen.

Encountering the *Eternal* Jesus:
A PRACTICAL APPLICATION

Remember—these four steps, as explained more fully on pages 23–24 in the introduction, are suggested to help you apply this quality of Christ to your own life.

1. **EXPLORE:** Take time to meditate on this quality of Christ. Use Scriptures in this chapter to get started.

2. **EXPERIENCE:** Turn your meditation into prayer that this quality might impact your life today. Pray the above prayer to begin.

3. **EXPRESS:** During your quiet time, take a moment to journal your thoughts, even if briefly.

4. **EXALT:** Pray, praise or even spontaneously sing your way through today's list of the names of Jesus. It only requires a few minutes.

GLORIFY HIS NAME

Every day I will praise you and extol
your *name* for ever and ever.

PSALM 145:2 NIV, *emphasis added*

Teacher and Master John 13:13 MSG

Teacher of Adam, The Psalm 94:10 MSG

Terror Laced with Glory
Judges 13:6 MSG

Tested Stone, A Isaiah 28:16 NIV

That Eternal Life 1 John 1:2 NKJV

That Spiritual Rock
1 Corinthians 10:4 NKJV

That Word John 12:48 MSG

Tower of Salvation, The
2 Samuel 22:51 NKJV

Towering Rock of Safety, The
Psalm 61:2 NLT

Trainer of Nations, The Psalm 94:10 MSG

Tried Stone, A Isaiah 28:16 NKJV

Triumphant Sword
Deuteronomy 33:29 NLT

True Bread from Heaven, The
John 6:32 NLT

True God, The 1 John 5:20 NLT

True Judge of All, The Psalm 75:6-7 TPT

True King, The Psalm 110:7 MSG

True Light, The John 1:9 NLT

True Mountain Guide Psalm 31:5 MSG

True Pasture Jeremiah 50:7 MSG

True Place of Rest Jeremiah 50:7 NLT

True Vine, The John 15:1 NIV

Truly Righteous 1 John 2:1 NLT

Ultimate Ruler, The Genesis 49:10 MSG

Unblemished, Sacrificial Lamb
1 Peter 1:19 MSG

Understanding Proverbs 8:14 NKJV

Unique One, The John 10:36 MSG

Unseen One Who Never Dies, The
1 Timothy 1:17 NLT

THE
INCOMPARABLE
JESUS

Exploring the Wonders of Christ's Greatness

> Everything about God is great, vast, incomparable. He never
> forgets, never fails, never falters, never forfeits His word. To
> every declaration of promise or prophecy the Lord has exactly
> adhered.
>
> A. W. PINK

SCOTTISH PRESBYTERIAN PASTOR, theologian and professor Samuel Rutherford (1600–1661) wrote of Jesus:

> Were there ten thousand millions of heavens created above these
> highest heavens, and again as many above them, and as many
> above them, till angels were wearied with counting, it were but too
> low a seat to fix the princely throne of that Lord Jesus (whose ye
> are) above them all.[1]

Some 21 centuries before Rutherford's birth in 1600, Ethan the Ezrahite (c. 539 BC) would seemingly speak in the Psalms of Rutherford's wearied angels when he wrote these words in Psalm 89:

> All heaven will praise your great wonders, LORD; myriads of angels
> will praise you for your faithfulness. For who in all of heaven can

> compare with the LORD? What mightiest angel is anything like the
> LORD? The highest angelic powers stand in awe of God. He is far
> more awesome than all who surround his throne.

PSALM 89:5–7 NLT

Everything Extraordinary

We come to the end of our journey together in spending a Month in
the Son. But the end of our journey is really just a beginning. There is
so much more of Jesus waiting to be discovered. I invite you to begin
again with Day 1 in this book. What a glorious habit—spending each
new day "basking in the Son"! But first we need to saturate ourselves
in a revelation of the *Incomparable Jesus*!

Incomparable, of course, immediately suggests that whatever you
are speaking about in using that word means nothing can compare to
it. A fuller definition of *incomparable* reads: "having no comparison or
no equal; matchless, unequaled, unmatched, unparalleled, unrivaled,
unsurpassable, exceptional, extraordinary, eminent beyond comparison;
not suitable for any comparison."

Christ meets any and all definitions, descriptions, adjectives, modi-
fiers or any other manner of descriptions when we speak of Him as the
Incomparable Jesus! Napoleon Bonaparte was clearly correct when he
said of Jesus: "Everything in Christ astonishes me! Neither history, nor
humanity, nor the ages, nor nature, offer me anything with which I am
able to compare Him and by which I am able to explain Him. Here is
everything extraordinary."[2]

Nothing but Jesus

In every way, Christ is supremely incomparable. No other religious
founder, philosopher, sage, prophet, statesman or any other hero or

heroine or historic figure is worthy of the worship Christ deserves. He is incomparable in His mercy, incomparable in His compassion, incomparable in His humility and incomparable in His beauty. He is, quite simply, incomparably unique. Indeed, Christ embodies the word *unique*: "One and only; having no like or equal; unparalleled; existing only in one known example." Christ alone is that "one known example." He is unquestionably incomparable!

Return with me for just a moment to review the encounter when three of Christ's apostles saw the Lord in His incomparable splendor on what theologians refer to as the Mount of Transfiguration:

> Jesus took Peter, James, and John and led them up a high mountain. His appearance changed from the inside out, right before their eyes. His clothes shimmered, glistening white. . . . Just then a light-radiant cloud enveloped them, and from deep in the cloud, a voice: "This is my Son, marked by my love. Listen to him." The next minute the disciples were looking around, rubbing their eyes, seeing nothing but Jesus, only Jesus.
>
> MARK 9:2–3, 7–8 MSG

The apostle Paul would later see Christ in a similar dramatic encounter on the Damascus Road when his name was yet Saul. Until that moment, he was a feared persecutor of Christians. *The Passion Translation* describes that moment: "Just outside the city [Damascus], a brilliant light flashing from heaven suddenly exploded all around him. Falling to the ground, he heard a booming voice say to him, "Saul, Saul, why are you persecuting me?" (Acts 9:3–4 TPT). So powerful was that moment that Saul was left blind for three days. Thus would begin one of the most remarkable conversions in the history of the Church. Saul had encountered the *Incomparable Christ*! He would soon become Paul, the chief apostle.

New Sights of Glory

Vital for every Christ follower to recognize is that there are new sights of glory to be discovered in spending intimate time daily with the *Incomparable Jesus*! He is all. He is everything. He is enough! Like the three invitees accompanying Christ into a "light-radiant cloud" atop a Judean mountain where their Savior was transfigured, may we have those moments when we, too, rub our eyes and see "nothing but Jesus, only Jesus!"

Return a final time with me to Paul's writings to the Ephesian Christians. In this letter, Paul speaks of how Christ has "raised us up with him and seated us with him in the heavenly places in Christ Jesus, so that in the coming ages he might show the immeasurable riches of his grace in kindness toward us in Christ Jesus" (Ephesians 2:6–7 ESV). Later in that same letter, Paul shares his personal testimony: "To me, though I am the very least of all the saints, this grace was given, to preach to the Gentiles the unsearchable riches of Christ" (Ephesians 3:8 ESV).

Two expressions leap from the text: *immeasurable riches* and *unsearchable riches*. *Immeasurable* means: "that which cannot be measured; boundless!" *Unsearchable* means: "that which cannot be searched; mysterious!" Together, those definitions, and all else we have shared on every page of this book, spells, for us, a single name—*Jesus!* Starting tomorrow, let's spend another Month in the Son!

A PRAYER FOR TODAY

Jesus, I thank You for the gift of this month, my personal Month in the Son, as I've basked in the wonder of Your incomparable presence.

Thank You for leading me through these 31 days, for encountering me in the midst of each of them, as I've explored new wonders of Yourself and Your heart to me. I pray, my incomparable Lord, that I might carry this habit of practicing Your presence forward into my everyday life. May I become increasingly aware of Your awesome greatness daily! I long to discover new wonders about You continually. Oh, how incomparable are Your great names! They are for me a continual feast for joyful worship and reflection. They remind me there is so much more of You to know. Keep me knowing. Keep me exploring. Reveal Yourself to me afresh each day. There is truly none like You! Amen.

Encountering the *Incomparable* Jesus:
A PRACTICAL APPLICATION

Remember—these four steps, as explained more fully on pages 23-24 in the introduction, are suggested to help you apply this quality of Christ to your own life.

1. **EXPLORE:** Take time to meditate on this quality of Christ. Use Scriptures in this chapter to get started.

2. **EXPERIENCE:** Turn your meditation into prayer that this quality might impact your life today. Pray the above prayer to begin.

3. **EXPRESS:** During your quiet time, take a moment to journal your thoughts, even if briefly.

4. **EXALT:** Pray, praise or even spontaneously sing your way through today's list of the names of Jesus. It only requires a few minutes.

GLORIFY HIS NAME

Let them *praise* the *name* of the LORD, for his *name* alone is
exalted; his splendor is above the earth and the heavens.

PSALM 148:13 NIV, *emphasis added*

Unshakable God Psalm 18:46 TPT

Unspeakable Gift 2 Corinthians 9:15 KJV

Upholding All Things Hebrews 1:3 NKJV

Vine, The John 15:5 NKJV

Visible Image of the Invisible God,
The Colossians 1:15 NLT

Warrior, A Exodus 15:3 NLT

Way, the Truth, and the Life, The
John 14:6 NKJV

White-Hot Fire Malachi 3:2 MSG

Wide River of Protection, A
Isaiah 33:21 NLT

Witness to the People, A
Isaiah 55:4 NKJV

Wonderful Counselor Isaiah 9:6 NLT

Word-Made-Flesh, The John 12:48 MSG

Word of God, The Revelation 19:13 NKJV

Word of Life, The 1 John 1:1 NLT, NKJV

World's Light, The John 8:12 MSG

Your Bodyguard Psalm 34:20 MSG

Your Confidence Proverbs 3:26 NKJV

Your Everlasting Light Isaiah 60:20 NLT

Your Exceedingly Great Reward
Genesis 15:1 NKJV

Your Glorious Sword
Deuteronomy 33:29 NIV

Your Guardian God Psalm 121:3 MSG

Your Holy One Acts 2:27 NKJV

Your Keeper Psalm 121:5 NKJV

Your Personal God Isaiah 43:3 MSG

Your Sacred One Acts 2:27 TPT

Your Security Proverbs 3:26 NLT

Your Shade Psalm 121:5 NKJV

Zion-Dwelling God Psalm 9:11 MSG

NOTES

A Call to the Heights

1. Karl Barth, *Church Dogmatics, Vol. 4, Part 2: The Doctrine of Reconciliation* (London: T&T Clark International, 2004), 78.

A Month in the Son

1. All definitions are from *Webster's New World College Dictionary*, 6th ed. (2018).
2. A. W. Tozer, *Whatever Happened to Worship?: A Call to True Worship* (Camp Hill, Pa.: WingSpread Publishers, 1985), n.p.
3. Luis de Leon, *The Names of Christ* (Ramsey, N.J.: Paulist Press, 1984), 63.
4. Andrew Murray, *With Christ in the School of Prayer* (New Kensington, Pa.: Whitaker House, 1981), 73.

Chapter 1: The Supreme Jesus

1. John R. W. Stott, *The Message of Ephesians* (Downers Grove, Ill.: InterVarsity Press, 1979), ii.
2. Dietrich Bonhoeffer, *Dietrich Bonhoeffer, Witness to Jesus Christ* (Minneapolis: Fortress Press, 1991), 238.
3. Charles Spurgeon, *The Complete Works of C. H. Spurgeon, Volume 37* (Fort Collins, Colo.: Delmarva Publications, 2013), n.p.

Chapter 2: The Awesome Jesus

1. Jonathan Edwards, *The Works of Jonathan Edwards*, vol. I-I, rev. (Ingersoll, Ont.: Devoted Publishing, 2019), 78.

Chapter 3: The Beautiful Jeus

1. Robert Murray McCheyne, *The Life and Remains, Letters, Lectures, and Poems of the Rev. Robert Murray McCheyne* (New York: Robert Carter, publisher, 1847), 253.

2. All synonyms are from Charlton Laird, *Webster's New World Roget's A–Z Thesaurus* (Cleveland: Wiley and Sons, 2010).

3. Francis of Assisi, *The Christian Library* (New York: Thomas George, publisher, 1835), 606.

4. Thomas of Celano, quoted in Wayne Simsic, *Living the Wisdom of St. Francis* by Wayne Simsic (New York: Paulist Press, 2002), 17.

Chapter 5: The Human Jesus

1. Timothy Keller, *The Reason for God* (New York: Penguin Books, 2008), 123.

2. J. I. Packer, *Knowing God* (Downers Grove, Ill.: InterVarsity Press, 1973), n.p.

3. Henry Law, quoted in Calvin Miller, ed., *The Book of Jesus: A Treasury of the Greatest Stories and Writings about Christ*, ed. Calvin Miller (New York: Simon & Schuster, 1996), n.p.

4. Bishop Melito of Sardis, *Orthodox Christianity: The Theotokos* (Prof. Kenneth Onapolis, publisher, no city given), 42.

5. John Piper, *Brothers, We Are Not Professional* (Nashville: B&H Publishing Group, 2002), x–xi.

Chapter 6: The Divine Jesus

1. Novatian, *The Sacred Writings of Novatian* (Altenmunster, Germany: Jazzybee Verlag Jurgen Beck, no year given), n.p.

2. John Piper, *Don't Waste Your Life*, updated edition (Wheaton, Ill.: Crossway, 2009), 37, 39.

3. C. S. Lewis, *Mere Christianity* (New York: Geoffrey Bles UK, Macmillan Publishers, div. of HarperCollins, 1952), n.p.

Chapter 7: The Obedient Jesus

1. Henry Blackaby, *Experiencing God* (Nashville, Tenn.: B&H Publishing, 1976, expanded 2008), n.p.

2. John Piper, *Desiring God: Meditations of a Christian Hedonist* (Colorado Springs, Colo.: Multnomah, 1986), 135.

3. Brother Andrew, *God's Smuggler* (Grand Rapids, Mich.: Chosen Books, 1967), n.p.

Chapter 8: The Suffering Jesus

1. Eugene Peterson, *God's Message for Each Day: God's Wisdom from the Word of God* (Nashville, Tenn.: Thomas Nelson, 2004), 101.

2. Matthew Henry, *Zondervan NIV Matthew Henry Commentary* (Grand Rapids, Mich.: Zondervan, 1987), n.p.

3. C. S. Lewis, *The Problem of Pain* (United Kingdom: The Centenary Press, 1940), 89.

4. John Piper, *Don't Waste Your Life* (Wheaton, Ill.: Crossway, 2003), n.p.

Chapter 9: The Resurrected Jesus

1. Hilary of Poitiers, *Ancient Christian Devotional* (Downers Grove, Ill.: InterVarsity Press, 2007), 99.

2. A. W. Tozer, *Mornings with Tozer, Daily Devotional Readings* (Chicago, Ill.: Moody Bible Institute, 1991), 98.

3. David Bryant, *Christ Is Now* (New Providence, N.J.: New Providence Publishers, 2017), 223.

4. Charles Wesley, "Christ the Lord Is Risen Today" (song, 1739).

Chapter 10: The Ascended Jesus

1. Bryant, *Christ Is Now*, 33.

2. Bryant, *Christ Is Now*, 33.

Chapter 11: The Humble Jesus

1. Charles Haddon Spurgeon, "Sermons Preached and Revised by the Rev. C. H. Spurgeon, Fifth Series" (New York: Sheldon, 1859), 20.

2. Andrew Murray, *Humility* (New Kensington, Pa.: Whitaker House, 1884), 11.

3. Murray, *Humility*, 12.

Chapter 12: The Compassionate Jesus

1. Mother Teresa, *No Greater Love* (Novato, Calif.: Originally published by Servant Publications, 1995, revised in 1997 by New World Library), 89.

2. Oscar Hammerstein, lyrics, "Sixteen Going on Seventeen (reprise)," *The Sound of Music*, 1959.

3. Mystic Teresa of Avila, quoted in Roger Housden, *For Lovers of God Everywhere: Poems of the Christian Mystics* (Carlsbad, Calif., Hay House Inc., 2009), 47.

Chapter 13: The Merciful Jesus

1. Lysa TerKeurst, *Unglued Devotional: 60 Days of Imperfect Progress* (Grand Rapids, Mich.: Zondervan, 2012), n.p.

2. T. D. Jakes, *T. D. Jakes Speaks to Men, 3-in-1* (Minneapolis: Bethany House, 2007), 507.

3. Charles Spurgeon, *The Treasury of David* (New York: Funk and Wagnalls, 1882), 316.

Chapter 14: The Abiding Jesus

1. O. Hallesby, *God's Word for Today: A Daily Devotional for the Whole Year* (Minneapolis: Augsburg Fortress, 1994), n.p.

2. Caryll Houselander, *This War Is the Passion* (New York: Sheed & Ward, 1941), 29.

3. Dwight L. Moody, "Where Art Thou?", *The Gospel Awakening* (Chicago: F. H. Revell, 1883), 400.

4. A. W. Tozer, *Experiencing the Presence of God: Teachings from the Book of Hebrews* (Minneapolis: Bethany House, 2010), n.p.

5. George Müller, "The Mighty God" (sermon) in *Jehovah Magnified* (Bristol, England: Bible and Tract Depot of The Scriptural Knowledge Institution, 1895), 104.

Chapter 15: The Spotless Jesus

1. Martin Luther, quoted in David Bryant, *Christ Is All* (New Providence, N.J.: New Providence Publishers, 205), 16.

2. Billy Graham, with Donna Lee Toney, *Billy Graham in Quotes* (Nashville: Thomas Nelson, 2011), 177.

3. Oswald Chambers, *My Utmost for His Highest* (New York: Dodd, Mead, & Co. 1935), n.p.

Chapter 16: The Missional Jesus

1. Oswald Chambers, *Bringing Sons unto Glory: Studies in the Life of Our Lord* (Grand Rapids, Mich.: Discovery House, 2015), 15.

2. Henry Martyn, quoted in Jason K. Allen, *The SBC and the 21st Century: Reflection, Renewal & Recommitment* (Nashville: B&H Academic, 2019), 42.

3. William Booth, quoted in Simon Guillebaud, *Choose Life: 365 Readings for Radical Disciples* (Grand Rapids, Mich.: Monarch Books, 2014), n.p.

4. Ion Keith Falconer, quoted in M. David Sills, *The Missionary Call* (Chicago: Moody Publishers, 2008), 181.

Chapter 17: The Authoritative Jesus

1. John R. Stott, "The Authority and Relevance of the Bible in the Modern World" (sermon), All Souls Church, London, 1979.

Chapter 18: The Praying Jesus

1. Thomas Goodwin, *What Happens When I Pray?* (Wyoming, Mich.: Grace Publications, 1998), 52.

2. Oswald Chambers, *Devotions for Morning and Evening with Oswald Chambers: The Complete Daily Devotions of My Utmost for His Highest and Daily Thoughts for Disciples* (New York: Inspirational Press, 1994), 621.

3. Dwight L. Moody, *Cyclopedia of Religious Anecdotes*, compiled by James Gilchrist Lawson (New York: Revell, 1923), 372.

Chapter 19: The Faithful Jesus

1. Graham Cooke, *The Language of Promise* (Lancaster, U.K.: Sovereign World, 2004), n.p.
2. David Wilkerson, *The Cross and the Switchblade* (Grand Rapids, Mich.: Chosen Books, 1963), 35.
3. Martin Luther, *Luther Gold*, comp. Ray Comfort (Alachua, Fla.: Bridge Logos Foundation, 2009), 50.
4. Charles Spurgeon, *The Treasury of David* (Pasadena, Tex.: Pilgrim Publications, 2016), 1111.

Chapter 20: The Miracle Jesus

1. Mother Basilea Schlink, *2017 Fall Quarter Evangelical Sunday School Lesson Commentary*, ed. Lance Colkmire (Cleveland, Tenn.: Pathway Press, 2017), 234.

Chapter 21: The Worthy Jesus

1. Augustine of Hippo, as cited by John Ankerberg and John Weldon, *Ready with an Answer: For the Tough Questions about God* (ATRI Publishing, 2011), 29.
2. Nathan Bierma, "Worship" article on Calvin Institute of Christian Worship website, June 24, 2005. https://worship.calvin.edu/resources/resource-library/worship-nathan-bierma/.
3. Bierma, "Worship."
4. Nikolaus Ludwig von Zinzendorf, quoted in David Butts, *Prayer and the End of Days: Praying God's Purposes in Troubled Times* (Terre Haute, Ind.: PrayerShop Publishing, 2009), 92.

Chapter 22: The Righteous Jesus

1. John Bunyan, *Grace Abounding to the Chief of Sinners* (Chicago: Moody Press, 1959), 81–82.

Chapter 23: The Selfless Jesus

1. Charles H. Spurgeon, *Morning and Evening* (New Kensington, Pa.: Whitaker House, 2001), 24.

Chapter 24: The Victorious Jesus

1. Watchman Nee, *The Word of the Cross* (Anaheim, Calif.: Living Stream Ministry, 1991), 14.
2. Watchman Nee, *Secrets to Spiritual Power: From the Writings of Watchman Nee* (New Kensington, Pa.: Whitaker House, 1928), n.p.

3. Ray C. Stedman, "When God Comes to Dinner" (sermon), January 1, 1968, www
.raystedman.org/old-testament/genesis/when-god-comes-to-dinner.

4. Alan Redpath (Sermonindex.net/Alan Redpath quotes), http://www.sermonindex
.net/modules/newbb/viewtopic.php?topic_id=5841&forum=34.

Chapter 25: The Joyful Jesus

1. S. D. Gordon, *Christian Advocate*, vol. 75 (Nashville: 1914), 32.

2. Robert Murray McCheyne, *Herald of His Coming* (Seelyville, Ind.: June 2015), n.p.

3. David Brainerd, *The Life and Diary of David Brainerd* (Readaclassic.com, publisher, 2010).

4. Sam Storms, *Pleasures Evermore: The Life-Changing Power of Enjoying God* (Colorado Springs: NavPress, 2014), 27.

5. Anonymous. Included in songs compiled by Linda Renstrom Beddoe, *Gospel
Singer's Wordbook* (London: Oak Publications, 1984), n.p.

Chapter 26: The Returning Jesus

1. Alan Redpath, *Evangelical Sunday School Lesson Commentary 2013–2014*, ed. Lance
Colkmire (Cleveland, Tenn.: Pathway Press, 2013–2014), 166.

2. Redpath, *Evangelical Sunday School Lesson Commentary*, 166.

3. Alexander MacLaren, quoted in David George, *The Daily Thought Shaker* (Grand
Rapids, Mich.: WestBow Press, a division of Zondervan, 2014), 311.

4. *Field of Dreams*, directed by Phil Alden Robinson (1989, Universal Pictures).

Chapter 27: The Glorious Jesus

1. A. B. Simpson, *The Fourfold Gospel* (Orlando: Bridge-Logos, 2007), 318.

2. W. E. Vine, *An Expository Dictionary of New Testament Words* (Old Tappan, N.J.:
Fleming H. Revell, 1966), 152–53.

Chapter 29: The Preeminent Jesus

1. Helmut Thielicke, *The Waiting Father: Sermons on the Parables of Jesus* (Cam-
bridge, England: The Lutterworth Press, 1957), 89.

2. John Knox, quoted in Dave Earley, *21 Most Effective Prayers of the Bible* (Uhrichs-
ville, Ohio: Barbour Publishing, Inc., 2005), n.p.

3. Bryant, *Christ Is Now*, 118.

4. Charles H. Spurgeon, *2017 Fall Quarter Evangelical Sunday School Lesson Commentary,* edited by Lance Colkmire (Cleveland, Tenn.: Pathway Press, 2017), 388.

5. Vine, *An Expository Dictionary of New Testament Words*, 274.

6. Jonathan Edwards, quoted in Isabella D. Bunn, *444 Surprising Quotes about Jesus*
(Minneapolis: Bethany House, 2006), n.p.

Chapter 30: The Eternal Jesus

1. George Müller, quoted in Roger Steer, *Delighted in God* (Tain, Scotland: Christian Focus Publications, 1997), 227–228.

2. Lewis, *Mere Christianity*, n.p.

3. Dietrich Bonhoeffer, *The Cost of Discipleship* (Munich, Germany: Chr. Kaiser Verlag, 1937), 61.

4. Max Lucado, *Grace for the Moment: Inspirational Thoughts for Each Day of the Year* (Nashville: Thomas Nelson, 2000), 180.

5. Lewis, *Mere Christianity*, n.p.

6. David Brainerd, *Memoirs of the Rev. David Brainerd* (New Haven, Conn.: S. Converse, 1822), 78.

Chapter 31: The Incomparable Jesus

1. Samuel Rutherford, *Joshua redivivus: or, three hundred and fifty-two religious letters* (Glasgow, Scotland: Andrew Young, 1824), 349.

2. Napoleon Bonaparte, quoted in R. W. Mills, *Truth—Not Exactly: A Book for Truth Seekers and Those They Care About* (Bloomington, Ind.: AuthorHouse, 2004), 372.

Dr. Dick Eastman is the international president of Every Home for Christ, a ministry that has planted over 4.5 billion Gospel messages home to home worldwide since 1946, resulting in over 240 million followed-up decision cards and responses and nearly 400,000 church fellowships called Christ Groups.

In his role with Every Home for Christ, Dick has traveled around the world more than one hundred times. He also serves as president of America's National Prayer Committee, a diverse group of evangelical leaders instrumental in planning America's annual National Day of Prayer (scheduled by Congressional decree for the first Thursday of May each year). As president of the National Prayer Committee, Dick has been invited to the White House as the guest of former presidents Ronald Reagan, George H. W. Bush, Bill Clinton, and George W. Bush.

Dick is the originator of the Change the World School of Prayer, a multipart seminar that has trained more than three million Christians in 120 nations on the power and intimacy of prayer. He is also the author of numerous bestselling books on prayer and evangelism, including *The Hour That Changes the World* and *Look What God Is Doing!*, which have sold more than two million copies worldwide.

Dick Eastman and his wife, Dee, make their home in Colorado Springs, Colorado, and have two grown daughters and nine grandchildren.

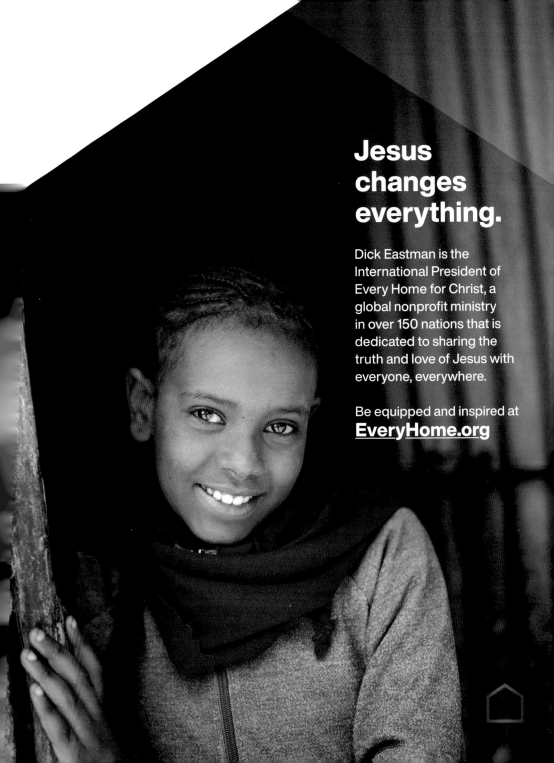

Jesus changes everything.

Dick Eastman is the International President of Every Home for Christ, a global nonprofit ministry in over 150 nations that is dedicated to sharing the truth and love of Jesus with everyone, everywhere.

Be equipped and inspired at
EveryHome.org